What God Said to the Rose

A guide to natural spirituality

Vincent Cole

ISBN-13: 978-0692231289)

ISBN-10: 0692231285:

 This book is intended for the development of individual spiritual abilities, to encourage, strengthen and enhance understanding of life on this planet. **The author and publisher assume no responsibility for any person or organization which uses the information unwisely.**

Library of Congress Control Number: 2014942617

Printed in the United States of America

"What God said to the rose,
causing it to laugh
and blossom in full-blown splendor,
was said also to my heart
making it a hundred times
more beautiful."

—Jalaluddin al-Rumi

What God Said to the Rose

CONTENTS

What God Said to the Rose

INTRODUCTION

The Symbol of the Rose

Behold the rose in its quiet splendor draped along a weathered wall of stone, climbing over a trellised entryway, or languid in a glass vase elegant in muted sunlight. Some people will pass by without noticing. Others will give it a quick glance and hurry on. A few will stop for a moment drawn by its splendid color and fragrance.

But a rose is more than a rose to those who have contemplated the depths of its color, venerated its distinct perfume and risked the bite of its thorns. Hidden within the folds of its petals, the rose embraces ancient dreams and current hopes. The rose is a living vessel containing the emotional yearning, boundless imagination and evolving spiritual progression of humanity. The symbol of the rose, an icon as alluring as its fragrance, makes it the most enduring and endearing of all flowers.

Throughout the centuries, the rose was, and still is, venerated in poems and honored in song, its likeness sketched, painted and embroidered, its aroma coveted and imitated, its form duplicated in silk, chocolate and precious metals. And yet, the rose began as just another flower struggling to survive. The earliest fossilized roses indicate that a simple, five-petal rose blossomed more than 35 million years ago. Though other flowers became extinct, the rose persisted and flourished long before humans appeared on earth.

To survive, thorn-like prickles protected it from prehistoric herbivores. To multiply, the rose sent out lateral runners producing new shoots, and used its color and fragrance to attract pollinating insects. The rose continued to spread upon the earth as birds carried away its fruit-like seeds. It truly began to flourish, however, when humans first saw within the rose a reflection of their own souls.

As civilization developed, so did the rose. The Chinese, for example, cherished it. They cultivated varieties such as Tiny Jade Shoulders, Clear Shinning and Three Rays of Dawn. At one time roses were so popular in China their cultivation encroached onto land needed for food production. The passion for roses was so widespread a Huang Dynasty Emperor was compelled to issue an edict limiting the size of rose gardens for fear the people's fondness for the flower would lead to famine.

In ancient Greece, the rose was considered a masculine flower. Rose garlands decorated the shield of the victorious Achilles while the goddess Aphrodite anointed with precious rose oil the corpse of the vanquished Hector. During feast days in Athens, naked youths crowned with roses danced in the temples dedicated to Hymen, the god of weddings. Devotees of Adonis grew exceptionally beautiful and fragrant roses in silver pots, believing their scent kept illness away.

In Egypt, fountains of rosewater perfumed the air. Rose petals piled knee deep carpeted the floors of Cleopatra's palace. Wreaths of roses accompanied mummies to their tombs.

It was the Romans, however, who were particularly obsessive. As in China, so avarice was the Roman passion for roses its cultivation began to encroach upon farmland. When winter came and the fields were fallow, tons of roses were imported from Egypt at a considerable price. The cost threatened to bankrupt the empire until the Romans invented the heated greenhouse to extend the growing season.

For the well-bred Roman citizen, roses were more than just an idle luxury. They were a necessity. They required roses to flavor their wine and food. Noble women used poultices of rose petals in the attempt to banish wrinkles. White doves, their wings anointed with rose oil, flew overhead at banquets. They draped garlands of rose blossoms on marble statues of their gods. Returning war heroes were crowned with roses while petals thrown from balconies fluttered in the air. The young Emperor Heliogabalus (202 - 224 AD), following the fashion of his time, showered his dinner guests with so many roses that several of them suffocated under the deluge. No doubt, the tombs of the unfortunate dinner guests were also mantled in roses, it being the custom for wealthy noblemen to have entire rose gardens cultivated for the sole purpose of keeping their mausoleums decorated. For the dead of lesser means, offerings of rosebuds during the Festival of Rosalia had to suffice.

The rose was life to the Romans and the poet Annius Florus reminded his fellow citizens, to pluck the full *rose "whose race will be run before the next setting of the sun. Gather it quickly before its glory is over."*

When the glory of the empire faded, it left behind a tarnished rose, a remnant of Roman rule, a symbol of decadent excess. Early church leaders shunned it, even tried to forbid its use but the rose endured. During the Middle Ages, the five-petals of a red rose became a symbol for the wounds of Christ crucified. Eventually the rose was transplanted to represent the Blessed Mother Mary. She became, as the poet Christina Rossetti would write hundreds of years later, *"Herself a rose, who bore the Rose. She bore the Rose and felt its thorn."* Litanies in her honor proclaimed her La

Rosa Mystica, the thornless rose and the rose garden of heaven.

One particular litany became known as the rosary, from the Latin word rosarium meaning rose garden. There are several legends claiming the rosary's origin. One story tells of a monk who recited his daily prayers while working in the monastery garden. In a vision, he saw his prayers become a garland of roses presented to the Queen of Heaven.

As the laity adopted the practice, kneeling on the cold floors of cavernous cathedrals and counting their prayers on beads of pressed dried roses, the setting sun touched them with petals of multicolored light shining through the rose window high upon the western wall. The rose window in full blossom with intricate tracery framing colored glass of dark ruby red, Chartres blue, smoky amber and muted purple, was a portal leading from a world of heavy stone and binding mortar to a radiant realm of beckoning brightness.

It wasn't only Christians who saw the rose as a symbol of the Divine. Islamic mystics see the flower as a representation of perfection, as well as an allegorical reference to Allah. Sufi poets, notably Jalaluddin al-Rumi, saw within the rose, its petals gently unfurling in a circle, the inner path guiding the soul to the core of all that is sacred.

Rumi wrote: *"In the driest, whitest expanse of pain's vast desert, I lost my sanity and found this rose."*

The true symbol of the rose is found in its fundamental nature, that essential quality which makes it unique among all flowers. Certainly, there are other flowers as fragrant and there are flowers some people say are more beautiful, but the rose is the most beloved because it shares a kinship with human existence.

From its simple beginnings, the rose has spread across the earth; blown by the wind, carried by birds and transplanted by human hands. Countless varieties blossomed and died, new forms are continually being born through natural evolution or human experimentation, yet the essence of the rose remains unchanged. Plucked from the ground, it became an extension of communication, an emblematic language of peace and war, of sworn secrecy and declarations of love but the true symbol of the rose remained cloistered and protected.

Centuries slipped by, empires fell and cultures withered away, yet the rose survived; its soul unaltered by the imposition of ancient myths, quaint fairytales and dogmatic beliefs now long forgotten.

The true symbol of the rose is revealed to those who take the time to look.

The true meaning of the rose can be seen growing wild along a roadside or trellised against the wall of an old churchyard. The inner meaning of the rose may be discovered in a bouquet bundled with baby's breath surrounded by ferns and tied with ribbon or suddenly the symbol is revealed by a single rosebud placed upon a casket lowered into the ground.

Those who stop to ponder the essence of the rose will soon discover its message. Once found, the message of the rose unfolds like petals opening in the sun. To understand it, to realize its full meaning, however, the soul of the rose must grow in the secret garden of the heart.

Chapter 1 The Rose Remembers

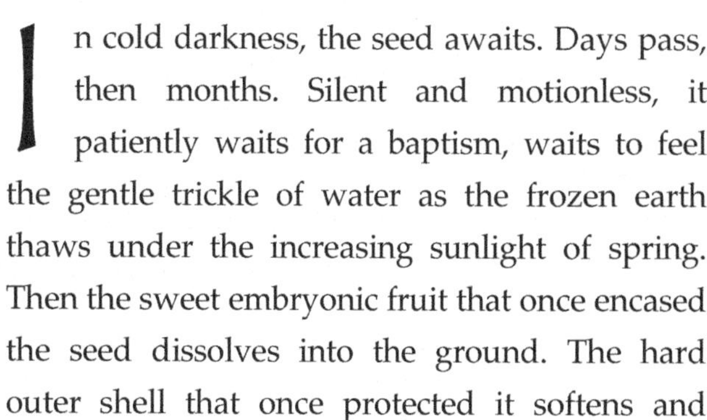

In cold darkness, the seed awaits. Days pass, then months. Silent and motionless, it patiently waits for a baptism, waits to feel the gentle trickle of water as the frozen earth thaws under the increasing sunlight of spring. Then the sweet embryonic fruit that once encased the seed dissolves into the ground. The hard outer shell that once protected it softens and splits open, releasing the seed to begin its journey.

The seed, exposed to the elements, vulnerable to the forces of nature, has no choice. To become a rose, to fulfill its potential, it depends on the world around it. It needs the earth, water, sunlight and all that nature provides so it can blossom and reveal its true beauty. Unless it abandons its shell and become receptive to the world around it, the seed remains small, hard and insignificant; its potential never realized, its true nature never revealed.

When touched by the elements, however, cells divide and multiply. Each cell knows its function. Thick roots grow and probe deep into the ground anchoring the seed to the earth. Thin feeder roots spread out seeking needed nutrients. Phosphorus penetrates the roots unlocking the rose's genetic memory. Potassium stimulates enzymes helping the rose to grow. Nitrogen, essential to all life on earth, encourages the rose to synthesize and transfer energy where needed.

Nursing on minerals and trace elements, a seedling pushes through the hard soil, feeling the warmth of the sun and the touch of a gentle breeze for the first time. It looks much like any other plant, a fragile sprout with two small leaves, its existence precarious. Not all seedlings will survive. Some may grow but never blossom.

The same forces that nourish the rose can also destroy it. An abundance of water will cause the roots to rot. Too much phosphorus and leaves turn yellow. Too much nitrogen and the rose may never flower.

The delicate balance needed to become a rose is so complex it is a wonder there are any roses at all. Still, they manage to not only grow, but also flourish in spite of extreme temperatures, drought, floods, fire and war.

The oldest among them is a rose tree believed to be more than 1,000 years old growing against the wall of St. Mary's cathedral in Hildesheim, Germany. An ancient legend tells of a king who lost a sacred relic while out hunting. After a long search, his soldiers finally found it hanging on a wild rose tree and the grateful king ordered a cathedral built alongside the rose.

During World War II, the cathedral was severely damaged by Allied bombing and the rose tree caught fire. Its root system, however, was undamaged. The ancient rose tree was born again as branches pushed through the rubble and its flowers bloomed in the midst of devastation. To the townspeople, it was a sign of hope and renewal.

The largest rose is a bush growing in Tombstone, Arizona. Its trunk is almost six feet in diameter and its branches spread over 8,000 square feet. Its taproots reach deep into flooded mines beneath the town, according to one theory. In full bloom, it displays more than 200,000 white roses.

Both the oldest and the largest began as small seeds patiently waiting in the dark. Each seed sought what it needed. They could not exist without the help of forces beyond itself. Though each seed contained the genetic memory of its true form, it took the power of nature to unlock the sequence of formation from seed to flower.

So it is with the creation called humanity. Every individual begins existence in the darkness of the womb when two distinct forces merge into one, initiating a chain reaction of cell formation. Neither of the two forces can accomplish this transformation on its own. It must lose itself in the other to become something greater. Within the womb, physical existence takes on form according to the collective genetic memory imparted by the two forces of its parents.

How well it develops depends on many factors, such as inherited attributes, proper nourishment and the vigor of its environment. From its conception, the human form is dependent on outside forces in order to exist. It will always remain dependent.

Nothing can exist on its own, but relies on all that surrounds it. The moon in its present shape exists because of its relationship to the earth. The human body depends on the earth to sustain it and the earth is able to provide because of its relationship to the sun. All forms of creation are linked with each other in an intricate interplay of complimentary and opposing forces constantly influencing and transforming each other.

All of creation, from the oldest rose to the newborn child, is in a state of continual transformation. Nothing remains stagnant. Nothing remains unchanged. The universe is in constant motion. Movement generates change. The rose blossoms, goes dormant then awakens as the seasons change according to the earth's orbit around the sun. An infant becomes a child, then an adult, then leaves behind the physical body and transforms into something greater. In constant motion, continually changing, all forms of creation seek to realize their full potential and express their true nature.

The true nature of the rose already exists within the seed. In order to fully become what it was created to be, the seed of the rose must break free of its small existence and breach the darkness to reach the world above. To express itself in all its glory, it must be more than a meager seedling content with a few leaves. It remembers there is more. Throughout its life, the rose will seek out and gather unto itself energies that encourage its inherent beauty, color and fragrance.

The memory of the rose is wide and deep. It reaches back through time, back to the origin of its species and all the variations of roses that ever existed. The rose will remember and build upon that memory, adding its own experience as a rose, contributing both its strengths and weaknesses for the benefit of future generations.

It is the same with humanity. Every person has complex memories like the elaborate, intertwined roots of a rose with thin roots stretching along the surface and strong, thick roots growing deep within the earth. Though grown at different times and at different stages of development, all memories are interconnected, always active and constantly accumulating and imparting information.

As the conscious mind shifts with every change in daily life, no matter how minuscule or momentous, so does memory unceasingly transfer information along a multilevel system that encompasses the entire being of an individual. The mind, the emotions, the muscles and bones, every cell and every atom holds the memory of a person's life on earth.

Consider the simple act of writing your name. The hand moves effortlessly across the paper, remembering every motion it takes to create your signature. You have no need to stop and remember how to form the letters. You don't even have to be thinking of your name. Your hand remembers what to do.

What once was studied and memorized is soon incorporated into automatic physical recall. This allows cerebral memory to concentrate on additional information, such as the time and place of an appointment, a new task to learn or a list of things to accomplish before the day ends. These memories are like ephemeral roots that grow when needed, then wither away when the information is no longer useful. Short-term memories can be discarded or the data shifted to another level to be held in reserve for future use.

Below those temporary roots are well-established memories containing necessary information often learned through repetition: reading, writing, communication, math skills, names, and telephone numbers, information that comes automatically to the mind when needed. Should the information fall out of use, it is transferred to a deeper level and becomes more difficult to access, much like a foreign language learned in school; if not spoken on a consistent basis, it can be forgotten. With some effort, however, there is recollection.

Having this complex and highly developed memory was essential to human survival. Lacking the physical prowess of other mammals, humans needed to understand the world around them. Weapons for hunting, the use of fire, planting crops and understanding the cycles of nature were all the result of humanity's intellectual development and enhanced capacity to remember what it discovered.

Within every individual being, there is the genetic memory of humanity's genesis. This memory determines not only the unique physical abilities and traits that differentiate humans from other species, it also retains the history of human survival. This core memory of basic human endurance continues to influence and shape social interaction through ingrained memories that have become ritualized over the centuries.

It is why hunting continues as a sport in societies where hunting for food is no longer a necessity. Hunting is an instinctual urge rooted in early human development. That same survival memory continues in industrialized cultures where collecting objects give some individuals an emotional sense of security as it once did when gathering and storing food meant surviving a long harsh winter. Another ancient remnant memory is the need for allegiance to a particular culture, country, work group or family unit. The "safety in numbers" mentality is an outgrowth of communal patterns of tribal cooperation. A solitary human rarely survived in prehistoric times.

Realizing how an ancient memory continues to have an impact on human civilization, consider how much more an individual's personal history influences his or her daily life. Every moment leaves its imprint; rooted in shadowy memory, almost forgotten until awakened by the smallest thing such as a faded photograph or dusty memento. A word, a gesture or an object can trigger if not a conscious recollection then a reaction similar to the original event.

When that happens, a harsh word becomes every harsh word ever spoken. One insult is every insult. One disappointment becomes every failure. Likewise, the memory of joyful events reverberates in the need to recapture those moments. Birthday celebrations, family gatherings and festive holidays become personal traditions if they were important events in the past. Conversely, people tend to avoid situations they associate with past unpleasant events.

Memory guides the individual on his or her journey in physical reality by storing and categorizing the different experiences of life as either pleasurable or painful, a reward or punishment.

These associations made in the past shape a person's self-image and outlook on life. A harsh childhood can lead to a life of defensiveness, an attitude that life will always be a struggle. The opposite extreme is how a pampered, comfortable life can generate a reality of personal isolation and self-indulgence. Both result in a self-created, limited reality, a lifestyle based on past associations.

There are, of course, variations within the perimeters of childhood experiences. As two roses grown under the same conditions will be different, variations in human personalities depend on the response, either positive or negative, to events pleasurable or painful, which occurred during the early formative years of a person's life. Just as the shape, color and fragrance of a rose is determined by its environment, much of an individual's personality and actions are shaped by old memories on its initial formation.

How memories influence a person's life is best understood by considering the fact that amnesia not only blocks access to personal memories, it also prevents a person from imagining a future. For instance, a person with amnesia cannot imagine a family gathering to be held the next day if there is no memory of ever having a family or ever attending a gathering. A future event cannot be envisioned without a past reference to draw upon.

Try this: imagine something is to happen in the future. Make it as elaborate or simple as you like—preparing a meal, attending a wedding celebration, shopping, driving to work. The moment you begin to imagine the event your mind retrieves incalculable bits of information from your memory in order to create a vision of the future. Take this experiment a step further by trying to imagine being in a small, obscure city, a place you have never seen, not even in a picture. All you could possibly do is create an image based on other places you have seen but it would be a false image.

Now consider how much of your present and future life is created and limited by experiences of the past. Anything without a past reference would seem false to you. Personal memories are building blocks in an individual's life. What you build depends on how those memories are used.

Memories, ancient and personal, can be powerful tools and yet human memory can be as fragile as the tender roots of a seedling. In spite of its amazing ability to compile and distribute countless bits of input, memory is not absolute. Memory is organic, a mutable energy that can be dynamic or feeble. It stores and discards information with an almost whimsical tendency. An important date is forgotten. An image of a childhood toy is recalled with great clarity. Someone's name suddenly slips away. Time or trauma alters memory and the distant past becomes more vivid than recent events.

Like the roots of a rose, memory can also be easily damaged. Disease, physical distress or emotional shock can disrupt access to the memory's system. A person wakes up in a hospital bed, yet doesn't remember the accident. A heart stroke, even for a brief moment, prevents blood and oxygen reaching the brain and a simple task like sitting in a chair is a challenge because the individual cannot recall the physical sequence it takes to sit. The memory of how to sit remains with the individual, however, the damaged brain is unable to access that particular memory.

All experiences, great and small, leave a remnant memory. The memory is never gone even when the ability to remember has withered. When the roots that retrieve those memories are blocked, it is an evolutionary safeguard to prevent any further physical, mental and emotional suffering. Repressing memories allows time and energy to focus on healing, rather than remembering and thus re-experiencing the original incident.

There is one root, however, that can never be broken. It is a memory that runs deep within all people. It may be forgotten. It may even be denied. This memory, however, can never be erased.

It is the original memory. Much like the thick, strong root that anchors a rose to the earth, this memory connects everything in the universe to the source of all creation. It is not some vague recollection of the ancient past, but the unending, intrinsic memory of how it was in the beginning, is now, and ever shall be. It is the living memory of God.

This original memory is a vital force. It flows in every cosmic cell. It's in the seed of the rose and the child in the womb. It lifts mountains beyond the clouds and gives birth to countless stars. And, when mountains crumble and stars implode, the memory of their existence merges with the original memory. Configurations of creation may come and go. All of creation has a beginning and an ending. The living memory, however, is eternal.

Nothing can erase the eternal memory of God. No force can ever destroy it. Yet, without nourishment, the root can weaken becoming a memory buried so deep it seems lost. Throughout human history, however, there have been individuals whose words and deeds served as a reminder. They lived on earth to awaken that deep memory and bring it into human consciousness.

Their message was simple: Remember the source of all life. Remember from where you came and where you will return. Remember your true nature.

From their simple message, religions grew. As religions became established, so did the weeds of arrogance. The simple message of teachers and guides was overshadowed by opinions impersonating as the word of God. Rather than encouraging the soul to blossom, the mandates of self-serving religions and rigid moral codes stifled the remembrance, robbing the soul of needed nutrients.

Yet, every religion is like an overgrown garden. Cut away the weeds and a beautiful rose is revealed, its roots deep and firm, drawing life from the primary memory of creation.

Within you, as well, is a dense garden jumbled with memories of the recent past, encumbered by experiences of childhood, cluttered with distracting concerns that eclipse the pure rose of your soul.

Deprived of light, the rose withers. Nevertheless, the root remains strong. Like the oldest rose tree on earth, still growing though scorched by fire and buried in debris, the rose of the soul can be born again. To resurrect the rose, to be truly born again, takes more than words or rituals. It is a lengthy endeavor to disentangle from the remnant memories of personal physical existence. Like a rose long grown in a small container, its roots bound in a tangled mass growing in circles, it takes a gentle touch and consistent effort to transplant yourself from a small limited personality to a greater understanding of yourself and a true appreciation of spiritual reality.

The process begins with the realization that you are not restricted by experiences of the past. Previous events in your life are merely that—momentary episodes. You are, however, more than a collection of memories. The experiences of physical life are events that occurred during the soul's journey on earth. Yes, they did influence you, but they cannot trap you in a cycle of repetitive reality based on residual memories. If only you would let them go.

Begin by sitting quietly and allowing yourself to remember. Look objectively at whatever memories arise as if they happened to someone else. If a memory is charged with emotion, whether painful or cherished, loosen the attachment with the words and realization, "That was then; this is now."

As emotional attachments to physical events loosen their hold, a deeper memory arises. Start to remember that before there was flesh and bone there was the soul. The memory is there, just as the soul is eternal even when obscured by the images and sensations of earthly existence. The memory is always with you, always a part of you just waiting to be remembered.

The soul holds the memory. It remembers the genesis of life, the breath of God that is all around you. When you are free from the constraints of physical memories, the recollection of the soul shines like a light illuminating the complexity and splendor of creation. The light of the soul reveals your perfect true nature loved by God as an intrinsic and cherished manifestation of divine creation. You existed before you took on physical awareness. You were born by a force greater than anything imaginable.

The human mind cannot envision an existence beyond its own physical senses because it remains focused on a reality created by its own collective memory. Human society with its struggles, fears and ambitions are still rooted in the earliest memory of physical survival. Though humanity has become the dominant species on the planet, it still sees itself as threatened by everything around it and so reacts accordingly. Humanity still creates a reality of conflict based on experiences of self-protection. Human existence is a self-perpetuating, self-created reality based on primitive memories.

Yet, the blossoming of the soul on earth is also part of the human experience. It is why religions have played a major role in all cultures throughout history. Religious works of art, music, scripture, sutras, and a multitude of rituals have all been a reflection of that initial memory. All are expressions of the soul's remembrance of God.

The memory of the divine nature of creation is within you. It has always been a part of you. This may be difficult to understand when the mind is preoccupied with physical desires. You are, however, more than a physical body. Truly, it has been said, "Man doesn't live by bread alone." The life of every individual is greater than the physical body, greater than the thoughts, emotions and actions of human expression.

Life is greater. Creation is limitless and unending. The human intellect can only perceive its own infinitesimal part of the universe. What the mind cannot conceive, however, the soul comprehends. It knows because the soul contains the eternal memory of God.

This soul memory is not of the mind. The human intellect is limited. Still, you can remember. After all, though you may not have knowledge of botany, nevertheless, you can respond to the beauty and fragrance of a rose. You can also experience the light and love of God without fully understanding God.

Just remember. Look beyond the world around you and nourish the deep root connecting you to all of creation and its creator. Let go of yesterday. It is over. See with fresh eyes. Hear with new ears. Feel with a new heart. It begins now.

The memories of the past will not be forgotten. Being born again is not a form of amnesia. The lessons of your life are invaluable.

Still, they were only experiences to educate, to enhance wisdom, not dictate who you are.

There is more to you. There is more to life. Begin to have new experiences in order to create a new future. Become born again in spirit.

All you have to do is remember.

Chapter 2- The Perfect Rose

It stands above all others, an ageless beauty unfurled in graceful symmetry. Its petals curl outward in smooth sensuous curves. Its fragrance is intense and intoxicating. Its color unsurpassed. Dewdrops glisten like liquid light. Deep green leaves branch in pleasant alignment along its strong straight stem. It is a most perfect rose. Other flowers vanish in its shadow.

This perfect rose has no thorns so you reach out to touch it, hoping in some way to possess its perfection. Your fingertips feel the delicate veins of each leaf and the velvet softness of every petal. Yet, things are not always what they appear to be and you discover the perfect rose is not a rose at all. What you hold is a manufactured replica made of molded silk, stiff wire and extruded plastic. The perfect rose is an illusion.

Perfection is a misconception, a synthetic quality invented by the human mind. It is a subjective opinion, an idealization never realized. Perfection is an avaricious weed in human consciousness spawned from judgments and beliefs made about the world. Perfection and its subspecies Superior, Special, Beautiful, Successful and Worthiness generate conflict, division and turmoil.

In order for something to be perfect there must be something that is imperfect. What is special can only exist when surrounded by, but separate from, what is considered simple, plain and ordinary. Physical beauty and social success are precarious classifications preferable to what is condemned as ugly and a failure. Yet, the prize-winning rose of today fades into obscurity tomorrow, no longer deserving honor and reward. Another rose is judged far superior, far more fashionable, and much more praiseworthy.

Worthiness is an offshoot of Perfection, an invasive weed that either gilds the rose in false self-importance or imprisons it in a strangling vine called Unworthiness that diminishes the rose's ability to blossom.

Look to the rose garden. There is no one true rose by which all others must conform. No single rose is favored by God over the others. The sun shines on each one. The rain falls upon every rose. The force of God's love is given equally to all. The rose of five petals does not envy the hundred-petal rose. The red rose does not condemn a rose of a different color. Wild flowers must run wild. Climbing roses must seek the heights. Each flower concentrates on fulfilling its own true form without seeking perfection, without judging itself or others. The rose with deep and wide roots freely accepting the pure water and nurturing earth and with outstretched, upturned leaves embracing the warmth of the sun will blossom forth in full radiance. Even the diminutive rose still struggling to secure itself to the earth basks in God's love.

To establish roots is to push past the weeds of misconception and feel what is all around you, to thrust through the confusion of worldly judgments and feel the force of God's love. One does not have to earn this love. One does not have to be perfect. Divine love is not a prize given as a reward. It is all around you. It flows throughout the universe, continuing to express itself in numerous forms, giving life but never dictating how life should be.

Consider the diverse forms of creation on earth, the mountains, valleys, the variety or roses, the leviathans of the oceans and the microscopic creatures of the air. Know that even more complex, ornate and diverse forms of life exist throughout the universe, some seen, others invisible to the human eye. Just as there are spectrums of light unperceived by the human eye and frequencies of sound beyond hearing, there exists unseen expressions of creation as much a part of life as roses and weeds.

Therefore, discernment is needed. Though all things come from God, not all are in harmony with God. There are those influenced by the light and those influenced by darkness. All created forms have the potential to mutate or evolve.

Within all expressions of creation is the capacity to nourish or deplete. There are forces that are of the light and forces that dwell in the dark.

Discernment is the ability to know the distinction, to see beyond appearances and distinguish the difference between a true rose and a manufactured artifice that appeals to the senses but not the heart. No matter how beautiful, how perfect in form and color, an artificial rose has a different vibration than a rose grown from a seed. Their energies are dissimilar. You have to experience each one to know the difference. Feeling and understanding the imitation, as well knowing the vibration of a true rose brings knowledge. Experiencing the warm, pure vibrancy of living rose in comparison to the dense, static energy of a reproduction teaches discernment.

Where there is a lack of discernment, deception thrives. The most harmless looking plant can be the most poisonous. Beautiful flowers can be deadly whereas an ordinary blossom may prove to be the most beneficial. Judging the worth of something based on appearances is ineffective. The conflict of what is deemed flawed and what is judged to be perfect is an illusion.

Seeking perfection fosters limited perception. The ability of the soul, however, perceives what the eye cannot see. Within each individual is an innate instinct which, when developed, becomes perceptive intuition, a heightened sensitivity to the various energies existing throughout the rose garden.

Trusting your feelings develops intuition. Feeling the energetic qualities and tone of an object or person or place reveals its true nature. Look deeper, not just with the eyes, but with the heart. See within yourself the rose that dwells within. See the rose blossoming within others, but do not ignore the weeds, do not be blinded by appearances.

Remove misconceptions so you can see clearly. Strip away the weed of wanting to be special, which separates you from creation. Do away with the manufactured imitations of beauty and success. Being worthy should not be questioned. You are a part of the rose garden and therefore worthy to receive its blessings. Turn away from the artifice of human opinion, speculation and judgment. Seek instead the natural force of God flowing throughout the universe.

Seek out the pure energies of existence. Seek and you shall find the clear waters of understanding, the ancient wisdom of the earth, the illuminating light of the sun.

Seek what is true. Find what is eternal.

Chapter 3 The Garden Path

Throughout the garden are numerous paths as varied and complex as the flowers surrounding them. Some are broad, heavily trampled highways. Others are solitary footpaths. Some are paved and clearly marked. Others are difficult to find, no more than faint imprints in the dirt. Some paths intersect, merge for a moment in time, then separate. Others are so closely parallel it's as if they were a single road.

Some roads expand and diverge in all directions like the branches of a tree. Others are narrow remnants of ancient trails paved with relics, bones and fragments of parchment. Some paths wait to be created, becoming a reality with the first footstep of an adventurous seeker yearning to learn the mysteries of the eternal garden and within its depths come to embrace its creator.

Every path offers a different and unique perspective. Each has its challenges and rewards. The greatest challenge is to find your path. You will need courage and determination. The most difficult part is taking the first step. When you discover a new path through the garden, you'll be stepping away from all you've been taught about the nature of reality. You'll be leaving behind a wide, well-traveled road that seemed safe and secure. Because it is wide and appears to be a safe, many people travel along this one road, believing it to be the only path through the garden. It's what they've been told. It's what they believe.

Nevertheless, the limitless extent of the rose garden is beyond human comprehension. It is more complex than imaginable, infinitely intricate beyond calculation. The garden cannot be imprisoned within the confines of human definitions. The garden is a living entity always changing, growing and transforming as it manifests all possibilities. It is the creative energy of God displayed in countless forms unencumbered by the limitations of time and space.

The garden existed before humanity stepped upon the earth and, as a creation of God, is not subject to human reasoning and control.

Divine Creation has its own rules impervious to the demands of human desires. In accordance to Divine Wisdom the earth shifts, fires rage, torrents of rain flood the soil as spiraling winds scour the landscape. The supremacy of natural forces demolishes prized possessions and obliterates mementos of the past. In an instant, everything cherished vanishes.

Though judged to be destructive and a threat to survival, dynamic expressions of nature are necessary. Life in all its aspects—the fire that purges, the water that rejuvenates, the earth that nurtures, the wind that uplifts—will always intrude upon illusions of a stagnant reality. Humbled by the forces of nature, people's long-held beliefs are revealed to be nothing more than a faded and fraying bouquet of artificial roses. Every flower, every mountain and ocean wave, every person and every creature walking upon the earth is subject to the cycles of creation, influenced and shaped by energies emanating throughout the universe. Nothing exists outside their influence. Nothing can inhibit the supremacy of God's creativity. Life cannot be limited within the boundaries of the human intellect.

A garden exists beyond the walls of the human mind, a garden of diverse yet harmonious patterns of beauty and wonder, each serving its purpose, each having a place in a complex, ever-transforming universe where no single form is more beneficial than another or, for that matter, less indispensable when creation begins to express another possibility.

Only one thing remains unchanged. To every person throughout time, there is an invitation to explore the way of the soul. It is a call to go beyond the wide road of sensory perception and physical sensations and take a path through twisting valleys, journeying into deep shadow and brilliant light, then climbing upward, spiraling to the top of a mountain to gaze upon a landscape of endless blue sky crowning a rose garden of eternal beauty.

With some people the invitation comes in an inexplicable persistent feeling that something is missing, a summons felt as a restless yearning for something more. Others may have a sense of alienation, of not quite fitting in with the ways of the world, feeling much like a stranger in a strange land.

Sometimes the invitation appears in a book such as this. Other times it comes in a sudden phenomenal vision wondrous to behold, or perhaps someone comes into your life, a stranger or a friend, who points to a new path outside the walls of your present existence.

Beyond the borders built stone-by-stone of learned perception and adopted beliefs, beyond all you think is reality, beyond all you see and hear, is a garden that surpasses all human hopes and dreams. Sometimes it takes an event of enormous intensity to crack the walls of limited perception and personal beliefs in order to see the far-reaching diversity and magnificence of the rose garden.

A death, an illness, a sweeping away of all that was known and cherished, is also an invitation. When personal security and safety are threatened, it is a call to step outside your boundaries, to seek more out of life, to search for what is real and everlasting, to find a different path, a new way to walk through the rose garden. When certainty and complacency are shaken, questions arise: How did this happen? Why? Is there more to life? Is there more to me? The invitation is in the answer: "Come and see."

The new path may be difficult to find at first. The dust of shattered illusions and the debris of broken beliefs may obscure it but the path is there. It has always been there. With patience and perseverance, you shall find it. Discernment will guide you. The first step is to confront your fear of the unknown. Once you have set your foot upon the path, your heart will know and your soul will rejoice.

Still, there will be challenges. Have faith that with every obstacle there will be assistance. With every ordeal, there is help. The garden is not a paradise and every path is designed to bring into your life those forces of creation needed to encourage the full blossoming of your soul.

Without faith, when natural and human-induced events upset the old road of illusions, those who travel upon it feel doubt and fear when personal beliefs are exposed as only imitation roses. Often there is a resistance to change. Many will yearn for stability and will struggle to have life as it used to be. They will dust off the artificial rose, trim its fraying edges and paint it a fresh color hoping it would last forever. But it won't last. All forms of creation must change.

The forces creating the universe, sculpting and transforming it, are neither a blessing nor a curse. They exist and will always exist in spite of human judgment. Each plays its part in the universe. It is only fear that divides these forces into beneficial blessings or ruinous disaster.

Consider the same flowers gathered as gifts to celebrate a joyful occasion are also the same flowers placed beside a hospital bed. The rose given as a pledge of love is pressed between the pages of a book then, years later, crumbles and is forgotten when love fades. The offering of a dozen red roses to mark an anniversary subtracts into one single rose resting on the grave of a loved one. Delightful or harsh, any personal judgment imposed upon the flower is an illusion

No matter where it is placed or how it is used, the rose remains always a rose. Cursing the rose will not change it. Praise does not improve its beauty. It remains only a rose, an expression of God's creativity.

Begin to understand this and you step away from the road of illusions. Do so carefully, but with determination and strength. With one small step, the sand will shift beneath your feet. The old road will crumble. Cracks will appear in its pavement and false images will splinter. With another step you'll begin to question your beliefs and discard those keeping you on a road not your own. Therefore, look beyond the illusions of a limited life. See past the façade and turn away from any imitation of a rose.

Seek and you shall find another way through the garden. As the old road fragments, another road will appear. A new direction will be revealed. Listen. A soft voice beckons. Your heart responds. A feeling arises—curiosity, yearning, an illogical impulse. You move forward with uncertainty.

Another step taken and the old road collapses in clouds of dust. You keep moving even though the new path is unclear. Cautiously, you place one foot in front of the other. Friends and loved ones call you back to the old ways of being. The echoes of their voices provoke confusion, doubt and fear. Many wanderers will heed their cries of alarm and return to the road of illusions. They will dismiss their glimpse of another path as a mistake and cling to what is familiar and seems safe.

Courageous and determined seekers, however, will hear and accept the invitation. They will face the hardship of sacrifice. The will find the strength to break down walls. They may stumble and fall, but they will rise again because they will follow the yearning in their hearts.

They will step forward knowing they can never turn back once they have glimpsed within the petals of a true rose, within all of creation, a reflection of their true self more beautiful than what was left behind.

Chapter 4 Entering the Garden

Imagine a vast garden where every variety of rose that ever was and ever will be grows in astonishing abundance. Seen from afar, it's a fusion of colors, a prism of floating hues overlapping and merging in chaotic beauty. Blood red and royal crimson blaze alongside roses colored like the dawn in tints of rusty orange and golden yellow. Scattered throughout the garden are roses in twilight shades of silvery lavender and pale amethyst. Above them are pillars of green foliage, some dark as the forest, some pale as jade, each carrying clouds of pure white blossoms. As you draw near, notice how some roses are more than one color: delicate cream-colored blossoms blushing pastel pink, earthy roses muted green with soft brown tints and fiery petals streaked orange and red.

Notice, as well, their different forms. Easy to recognize are the urn-shaped roses with their tight, overlapping petals. Some roses, spiraling outward, are cup shaped. Others look like pompoms. Among them are simpler forms: humble roses with open faces of five petals and the rare four-petal variety. In contrast, are round roses of a "hundred-petals."

Enter the garden and the fragrance of countless flowers surrounds you. With every step you take, there is a greater awareness, a heightened sensitivity to the subtle variations of perfume. In the air are hints of citrus, moss, tea and spice. The scent trembles on waves as you pass by roses with a strong bouquet, others with only a slight aroma and those without any scent at all. Let the perfumed air carry you along the garden path.

Wander aimlessly among the roses. See the bold 30-foot giants using their hooked thorns to lift themselves upon the branches of a tree. Seek out the shy ones, the miniature roses with buds no bigger than a grain of rice. As you walk among the flowers see how some stand upright while others creep along the ground. Notice how clusters of roses surge over walls. Others huddle together to form hedges and shrubs. Notice also how some roses grow wild and unhindered while others remain enclosed behind high fences.

Walk and watch. Observe the seedlings pushing through the dense soil. Further along the path, a flower withers and dies, its faded petals falling gently in the wind. Nearby, rose buds open to reveal their golden stamens in a segmented halo of brilliant color. Some roses you see will come into flower only once a year while others will bloom from spring to autumn. There are also roses that will never blossom.

Look with curiosity and wonder at the diversity of it all. Sense beneath your feet the ancient and enduring earth. Feel the warm rays of the sun and the cool mist of a distant waterfall. Look. Be aware. Observe life in the rose garden. So much diversity of shape, color and fragrance. Yet every one is a rose, everyone an example of the infinite possibilities of creation, every rose an expression of divine creativity flowing throughout the universe.

To judge even a single rose is to judge God.

Chapter 5 A Meditation

Read these words as if following stepping stones along an unknown path. Walk with diligence. Read with curiosity.

Follow with an open mind.

It is twilight, a time of transition as the sights and sounds of the external world begins to fade and internal life of the soul begins to awaken. The last gold and red light of sunset still shines brightly upon a narrow path leading into a forest. Birds with white wings fly overhead returning to their nests. A pale moon appears faintly on the dark blue horizon. A gentle breeze carries the scent of roses and pine trees. You feel a soft touch on your shoulders guiding you forward.

Though the path is narrow, it is straight and the ground beneath your feet is soft and yielding. Entering the forest, a blessing of pink petals from flowering trees fall spiraling in the air, sparkling like jewels in the last rays of the setting sun. They touch your face like a soft caress. They fall like a veil on your head and shoulders.

The forest welcomes you.

Stately trees stand as silent silhouettes in the fading sunset. The first few stars of night glimmer above the treetops. Sight and sound diminish in the stillness of the dim moonlight. All is quiet. Peaceful.

Nothing moves. There is no sound. In this forest, your physical senses won't serve you. Everything around you is just a vague outline hidden in shadow. If fear arises, breathe deep and let peace prevail. You have learned to rely on the five physical senses to guide you through life but physical abilities are undependable and limited. Just as there are frequencies in sound that cannot be heard and spectrums of light invisible to the human eye, there are forms of creation outside physical perception. Dependence on physical and mental capabilities restricts awareness.

You are more than a physical body. Life is more than what you can see and hear. Relinquish your reliance on physical experiences and another source of perception will manifest itself. Within you is the ability to recognize the multiple shifting vibrations of the forest. You can feel the life of the trees surrounding you: the green sapling with its small tender leaves, the ancient grey oak soon to fall, decompose and replenish the earth that once nourished it.

Let your soul, the eternal life force within you, reach out into the forest. It knows creation, the trees, the rocks, the towering mountains, the vast rose garden, not as something separate or dangerous, but expressions of God's love, each form according to its unique nature, each united, interacting and influencing the perpetual transformation of creation.

The soul discerns without seeing and perceives without hearing that the forest, even at night, silent and tranquil, continues to transform itself. Saplings quietly grow. Old trees shed their leaves. Boulders become pebbles worn down by the forces of wind and water. Shafts of silver light shift as the moon travels along its course.

With every step taken along the path, you are also transformed. Your body becomes more relaxed and lighter. It seems you are no longer walking but floating as if carried along, passing through moonlight and shadow. Be aware of rustling feathers as birds stir in their nests. Sense the fox dreaming in its den. Let your soul embrace the stars.

Float in the moonlight. Feel life around you. Every form of creation has its own distinct tone. The motion of atoms is music. Feel the deep bass notes of rock and earth. Experience the mid-tones of tree and rose. Let the aria of the wind engulf you. Be swept into the harmony of creation. Become part of the universal hymn. Dance to the song of God.

Without any effort you will be transported to a clearing in the forest so bright in the moonlight it looks frosted with snow. Your awakened intuition senses something, a particular vibration different from its surroundings, a solo voice calling out to you. In the distance, half hidden in the tall grass and wildflowers, something blue sparkles in the moonlight.

You are drawn to it. Step into the clearing. Dazzling brightness overwhelms you. Guided by your feelings seek the blue spark in the field of white, sense that one particular vibration from among all the others.

Seek and the soul will soon see a shimmering pale blue vague form pulling you closer. Concentrate. The color becomes stronger, deeper, and richer as if it possesses every shade of blue found in sea, sky and sapphires.

Your own desire to explore and discover urges you forward. It may be difficult at first finding the source as you learn to focus your newfound sensitivity and discern the vibration of blue in the midst of moonlight, but persistence will heighten your sensitivity and awareness. Therefore, continue to seek and you will find a solitary blue rose growing in the moonlit field. An impossible rose, none like it grows upon the earth. Attempts are made to produce a blue rose, but all experiments so far have failed. Nevertheless, it exists. The blue rose blossomed the moment you stepped upon the path.

It is a young flower and will need nurturing to grow strong. It will need attention and protection. If abandoned, it will wilt.

Gently lift the blue rose from the ground. Take it. Return it to its true home. There is only one place where it will blossom in full beauty.

Take the rose and place it in your heart.

Now feel its laughter and song
fill your soul.

Chapter 6 Transformation

Transported by wind, water and wings, the seeds of the rose scatter across the land. Some fall on fertile soil; others on rocky terrain. Some take root under a full day's sun while others struggle in the shade. Some seeds take root where water is plentiful. Others thirst where rain is scarce.

Every dwelling on earth is a challenge. Seasons differ from year to year. Rivers flood. Volcanoes erupt. The ocean engulfs the shoreline. The earth itself shifts beneath the surface. Creation is inconsistent: extreme and subtle, severe and mild. Nature follows a profound wisdom greater than the human desire for comfort and predictability.

The rose does not fear the wisdom of the earth. It surrenders to it. Through drought and flood, in sunlight and shade, the rose adapts to a changing environment by transforming itself rather than resisting the shifting conditions of the landscape. To do so, it must forsake the traits of its parentage and evoke a deeper memory of creativity and experimentation.

The challenge of a new environment releases within the rose an innate ability to transform itself by altering its growth pattern, forming petals in a way unlike its parent and developing a different color and fragrance. Horticulturists call this process a "sport." Whatever the term used——sport, evolution, mutation, alchemy—— it is nothing more than the fluid nature of creation expressing limitless possibilities in diverse and marvelous forms.

To walk a new path is to seek out and discover new possibilities within the rose garden, within life, within you. It is not an easy path. It is unlike any other road because it is your path, your journey. Though you may desire the path to be an easy voyage, nevertheless, there will be challenges.

Because it is unfamiliar, the way can be confusing as it meanders through the garden, sometimes up steep hills, sometimes across rocky soil and desert land. Because it is your road, taking you along a path of life so different from the one you left behind, it can be a lonely voyage at times. You will need strength to endure, devotion to persevere and faith to face the unknown.

Much will be given to you, but much will also be taken away. Like the pruning of a rose before new growth begins, old dead wood and branches that do not bloom will be removed. Beliefs that no longer serve you will fall in the light of new understandings. What once seemed so pleasurable will become empty. Old ways of doing things will become tedious and oppressive. Cherished friendships and established relationships will change. Even those branches, which have been grafted unto you, though beautiful and fragrant, will be cut down to the original rootstock so that you may return to your own true self.

Pruning away what is harmful or useless to the rose is surgery and can be painful. Growth and transformation requires sacrifice. Before new growth can begin, you will feel a sense of loss and a feeling of mourning. Your beliefs about yourself, your own sense of identity, will be radically revised.

As with all forms of life, forces of addition and subtraction shape you physically, mentally and emotionally. As the old way diminishes, new experiences, like a new environment, will bring forth new growth, encouraging creative self-expression and a transformation of form and identity. With each cycle of new growth, what is old, dried and useless must be pruned and discarded but with each new season, something beautiful emerges. It takes time. It takes patience. Most of all, it takes willingness.

By pruning the weak and diseased branches, energy is directed towards new growth. If neglected, the old contends with the new for the same energy source. Conflict arises and the rose will weaken. In its compromised condition, it may never blossom. So it is with individuals who seek change but avoid looking within. They cling to old traits, old ways of being. Illusions flourish. Limited beliefs constrict growth. They resist the challenge of altered circumstances and the lessons of new experiences.

But for those who take a different path, who seek another way, there is help. The entire universe, always creative, never stagnant, encourages your transformation. With every step along the path, buried abilities will surface and blossom. Your vibration will shift, become clearer, more open to life. A refreshing fragrance will surround you.

Brilliantly-colored blossoms will grow as stronger roots grow deep to seek the treasures of the earth and new branches with upturned leaves spread wide to receive the blessings of heaven.

Carried by the wind of spirit, swept by the water of renewal and lifted into the realm of sacred creativity, you begin an inner conversion allowing you to see and experience a reality far greater, more wondrous and beautiful than the human mind can imagine.

Chapter 7 - A Tale of Two Roses

Two seeds from one plant, by nature's fate, took root in different lands.

One grew under the protection of a greenhouse where it was given everything it needed. Time-released fertilizers consistently supplied food and so the rose never knew hunger. Scheduled watering was augmented with gel-like polymers that released moisture into the soil and so the rose never knew thirst. When storm clouds loomed overhead, automatic lights brightened and warmed the day so the rose never had to suffer the cold darkness. Even the air was enhanced with vapors of liquid carbon dioxide to encourage growth. In time, the rose blossomed.

Not far from the glass walls of the greenhouse, the other seed took root upon a hilltop. The land was poor and rocky. It had to dig deep through clay and gravel; its roots clinging to any good soil it found. With quiet endurance, it survived droughts and floods, scorching days and lonely frigid nights. When weeds threatened to overcome it, the rose spread its leaves and overshadowed them. When high winds blew dust upon it, tears of morning dew washed it clean and though it slept under winter's solemn frost, the rose always awakened to the first warming sunlight of spring and the music of songbirds welcoming the dawn.

The rose knew hunger and thirst. It felt the deepest darkness. Still, the rose grew and, with patience and determination, it blossomed.

Now consider this.

Of the two roses,

which one was the strongest?

Chapter 8 The Seasons of the Rose

When the seedling emerges,

when the first tightly curled bud appears,

when the rose comes into flower and releases its fragrance,

when brilliant colors that once blazed in sunlight become muted in the mist, when green leaves turn to bronze, then tumble to the earth,

when bare flowerless canes rise icy-black through drifts of snow,

when in full blossom or shedding the last of its withered leaves, the rose remains always a rose.

Roses naturally transform to harmonize with the greater wisdom of the earth. They submit to the rhythm of the seasons, adapting rather than resisting the natural forces of creation. Though they change form in accordance to different environmental shifts, roses never lose their true essence.

The soul also harmonizes with the forces of creation, the varying seasons of blossoming and relinquishing, of formation and demise. It adapts to the ebb and flow of energy during cycles of labor and rest. It surrenders to the greater celestial power flowing throughout the universe.

As you journey through the rose garden, you will discover different energies, some delicate like a falling leaf, some powerful as a sudden blizzard. You'll become sensitive to vibrations unlike anything experienced on a mere physical level. Along the new path, you will experience the seasons of the soul, seasons that can change from one moment to another, independent of clocks and calendars, uncontrolled by human strategies and self-imposed deadlines. The seasons of the soul emanate from God's creativity radiating throughout the endless universe, throughout time and space, throughout your existence in all its forms.

When you are an infant first awakening to the wonders of the world,

when as a youth discovering your potential,

when adulthood imposes responsibility and action,

when you feel the spirit within you and begin to blossom

when the winter of old age reminds you that the physical body is only a temporal dwelling place,

when you feel all these stages of life in one overwhelming moment, the soul still remains the essence of your existence.

Walking within the rose garden, discovering different expressions of God's creativity with each twist and turn in the road, is the journey of the soul. With the ever-changing seasons of the soul come new discoveries. Every discovery increases understanding and with enhanced understanding comes growth and flowering. When your awareness expands to encompass a greater vision of the rose garden, personal transformation begins.

All you have to do is walk the path and seek the wonders of the garden. The path itself will teach you. The seasons of the soul will guide you.

In springtime, the season of beginnings, the seedling bursts from its womb and puts forth its roots, it pushes through darkness to reach the sunlight. Though tender and vulnerable, nevertheless, it has the strength and determination to overcome any obstacles that would hinder its growth.

The springtime of the soul begins in some people with a subtle awakening, a restlessness or boredom with routine. It grows stronger into a yearning for something more in life, something different and unknown. With others, it comes heralded by a sudden event, an epiphany or an unexplainable persistent feeling. It is like the clouds parting for an instant and a ray of sunlight glows all around you. You sense its brightness flowing through you. You feel its warmth. It may only be for a fleeting moment and yet it feels like an eternity. You want more but clouds return.

Then you must find your wings. You must find the power of your soul. With wings outstretched, striking the air in rhythmic waves, you set forth a fierce windstorm scattering the clouds of confusion and doubt.

For the soul, springtime is the season of great effort. It is the season of struggle. Just as the rose begins to realize its potential by breaking free of the hard shell that once protected it, there is a struggle to break free of old beliefs and ways of being that no longer protect but entomb. The mind must break through barriers of limited perception just as a seedling thrusts through the dense, compacted dirt to break through the surface of the earth and reach the sunlight.

The young rose must also grow downward into the earth, pushing aside rocks and debris, finding nourishment in the soil to encourage growth. You must also go inward, overcoming emotional obstacles of fear and arrogance. You must also seek sustenance for the soul. Deep within you, once clear of the debris of obstinacy and complacency, you'll find the strength and wisdom to reach the light. Remember always, it will take effort. Though springtime is the season of growth, it is also a time of conflict and opposition. As the rose begins to grow, so do weeds and pests.

Weeds are forces in the physical and ethereal realm that fear change and resist growth. They see anything new, anything different as a threat to their own existence. Weeds will try to hinder your growth by keeping you in the shade, denying you the freedom to extend your roots and using negative energy to discourage any flowering. Pests are a variation. They are parasitic. They cling like a fungus, always taking, never giving. Their nourishment is whatever energy they can acquire. Using flattering words, invoking pity or instigating anger, they attempt to maintain an energetic bond with their host. In their mildest form, they are a distraction. At their worse, they can be exhausting; depleting your energy and distracting you from seeking the nutrition needed to grow.

With so much opposition, it is a wonder any roses survive. Yet, not only do they survive, they thrive. Wild hardy roses growing by the roadside, ancient roses rising from the ashes and towering roses that blossom over acres of land developed their strength and tenacity in response to hostile forces. Challenges did not hinder growth, but helped cultivate the rose.

The soul also develops during the springtime of birth and renewal by defying those forces that would attempt to frustrate and destroy. You have the strength of the soul and the power of your wings to overcome resistance. Furthermore, you are not alone in the struggle. Gardeners know that roses do especially well when planted alongside certain plants such as geraniums, garlic and marigolds. Companions in the physical and spirit realm also aid and protect you. They are like midwives assisting and comforting during the most difficult stages of birth.

A woman giving birth to a child has pain because her time has come; but when her baby is born, she forgets the anguish because of her joy that a child is born into the world. So it is with you.

Therefore, face the challenges of birth and growth with vigilance and determination. Find the strength of your own wings. With humility and gratitude, accept the help surrounding you. Be patient and endure. There will be a summer and there will be joy.

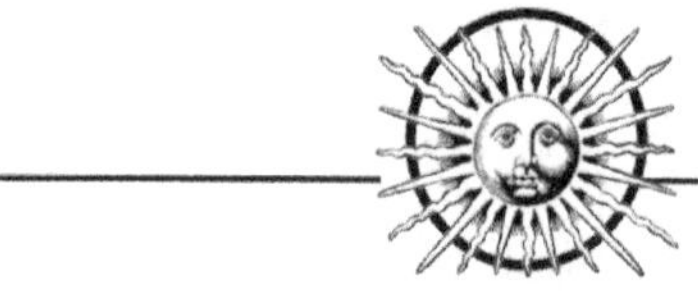

In the warmth of summer, the breeze is gentle. Rivers flow calmly to the sea. Flowers blossom. Burdens feel light. The soul is in its glory. When roots are firmly established, when leaves and thorns are in place, when neither flood nor wind can undermine, so begins the summer of soul, the season of surrendering and feeling at peace as the petals of the rose slowly unfold.

Summer is a time to relax and allow growth to develop naturally without effort, without struggle.

In quiet repose, the soul basks in the light, balanced between time and eternity, reaping the rewards of its endeavors. In summer, the soul receives what it needs. Tender rain falls when the soul thirsts. The bread of life is abundant when the soul hungers. Tranquility embraces the soul and protects it when clouds of turbulence threaten.

The physical body also benefits. Birth and growth can be exhausting, confusing and even painful. Summer is the time to slow down, to rest and recuperate. The body and mind need time adjusting to new energies, new ways of being, no longer stumbling forward but walking firmly upon a new path.

The soul needs to feel the power of its wings. Therefore, give to the world only what is necessary and give to yourself the time to relax. Close the garden gate against distractions and, as the saying goes, stop and smell the roses.

Allowing yourself personal time is not selfish. It is being wise. A fountain never replenished soon runs dry. The summer of the soul is for you, a time to turn away from the demands of others, the trivialities of the world and its endless activity. In summer, you listen to your soul and fill your heart.

Neither begrudge yourself the time nor seek to extend summer beyond its natural course. Clinging to an endless summer is self-indulgence. The summer of the soul lasts only as long as needed to maintain balance and encourage further growth. Seasons change. Days will seem shorter. Rose petals must fall.

Summer must bow and yield to autumn, the season of sacrifice when leaves and flowers wilt, descend and decay. Through decomposition, the sacrifices of the rose transform into nutrients that replenish the soil, thereby returning to the earth the gifts it received in summer.

When autumn comes, it calls upon the soul to give, to share the harvest. What the soul has received freely from God it must now give freely to all who would accept the gift. In autumn, the soul spreads its wings. One wing is called Wisdom, the innate knowledge of appropriate action. The other wing is Discernment, giving freely and yet, never bestowing pearls upon swine.

Beating in unison, the two wings lift you higher, giving you an expanded view of the rose garden. With outstretched wings, you begin seeing further than before, looking beyond your own personal boundaries and noticing, perhaps for the first time, a world outside your own personal needs and desires. Then you will realize that your challenges are everyone's challenges and your problems are the problems of many others. You will see your life as part of the human condition on earth. Now spread your wings. Rise to new heights. See the world around you.

In the distance, a wanderer is stuck in a labyrinth of his own design. He struggles to find a way out. Fly to him. Show him the path leading out of confusion.

Elsewhere, a seeker wanders in circles. Vines entangle her feet, holding her to the past. She doesn't understand why she can't move forward. Tell her. Share what you know.

Another one is lost in the shadows and she is sinking in sand. Go to her. The wing of Wisdom will guide you. Wisdom will caution you not to jump into the situation. Do not stand with her and be caught in the quicksand. Instead, stand firm and reach out. Stay on your path but lend a helping hand. Give of yourself, but do not give up yourself. Trust in your Wisdom.

The wing of Discernment also guides and protects. Discernment is not judgment. It is awareness, seeing people and events with clarity, seeing without condemnation, without judgment, not blinded by feelings of pity. Look instead with compassion and understanding.

Let the wing of Discernment guide you as to when you can help and when you must stand aside allowing events to take their course, knowing the lessons of life, painful as some may be, are happening for a reason.

Look and you will see many held in prison of their own making. Even though the bars are old and rusty, though there is a key in the lock and the prison walls are made of paper, they do not attempt to escape, but sit complacently calling out, "Have pity and help me," while whispering, "Join me in my prison and keep me company." Though they can walk, they do not rise. Though they have wings, they do not fly.

There is nothing you can do. Many are lost but do not seek while others seek another way but refuse to sacrifice that which holds them back. Fear of change chains them to the very things they wish to escape. Many will call out for help but will not hear the answer. Many see a new path but will not venture forth. Some are too comfortable in their prison cell and want others to share in their misery, using pity to ensnare others in a web of continual drama and conflict. They may claim to be weak, might even appear helpless but be forewarned; they have the strength to hold you captive.

Spread your wings and rise above such entrapments. To care for someone is to give the gift of a priceless pearl. Some will see and appreciate its value. Others, however, consumed by their own selfish hunger and blinded by illusions will trample the pearl into the mud. Therefore, seek instead those who are truly in need. The wing of Discernment knows if you are helping someone or merely aiding and abetting someone's illusions.

Help to give sight to the blind so they may see another way. Banish the cataracts of illusion. And, when their illusions fall like dry leaves and the illusions within you begin to disintegrate, know the season of winter is near.

When winter comes the whole world seems to stop. The sky is empty. The garden is silent. A few remaining birds huddle quietly in their nests. Bears hide in hibernation. Waterfalls, once wildly splashing in summer, slowly become jagged sculptures of ice. Sound is muffled, absorbed in drifts of snow. Trees are barren. Roses are only branches of thorns.

Winter is a time when deep silence prevails, water petrifies into ice, and light dims behind veils of grey clouds. Nothing moves. Nothing grows. It's as if the soul is suspended in ice. You feel numbed by frost. All endeavors seem blocked by snowdrifts. There is a feeling of emptiness in winter when fruit trees bear only strands of icicles. There is loneliness in winter, a sense of being isolated from God and humanity.

The winter of the soul is a time of death. Deep-rooted illusions wither. Long-standing attachments are broken and abandoned. Friendships fade. The heart grows cold and shatters. In the bleakness of winter, everything appears lifeless. In the darkness of winter, the old way is dying. It is a time of mourning.

The human mind fears the end of a treasured but limited reality and it cries out in anguish and shouts in despair. The mind yearns for the pleasures of summer. It attempts to preserve the flowers of spring, but the dried petals crumble to dust. All seems lost. All seems hopeless. The pain of winter seems endless.

But the soul is patient and at peace, knowing that winter is only a part of a cycle and death is only another illusion.

In time, spring will return. There will be a resurrection when warm breezes arise and grey clouds disperse. The sun's fire will again touch the earth, warming the soil, encouraging birth. The ice will thaw, waters will flow again and a newly formed heart will be stronger, wiser and more radiant once cleansed of winter's decay. Therefore, do not fear the pain of transformation.

Do not resist the suffering, the emptiness, not even the periods of boredom.

Accept the changing seasons. Embrace the blessings of heaven and earth. They will help you flower in full-blown splendor.

Chapter 9 Earth

Ancient is the earth and great is her wisdom. Though small and humble, her soil is rich with the history of transformation. She is a living record of endless cycles of death and rebirth. She is the planet of fire and ice, of devastating storms and cool summer breezes, of massive ocean waves carving new shorelines and mist-shrouded mountains silent and still in soft gray light.

The earth knows she is only a small part of the universe, a mere speck in the outer region of the galaxy and yet, she contains an ornate diversity of divine creativity——elephants adapted to living in the desert, luminescent creatures in the deep dark seas, the palm tree that blossoms once in a hundred years then dies, the fungus that lives on the roots of the rose helping it to endure.

The earth gives freely but never diminishes. She serves all but is subject to none. She tolerates mistreatment but never weakens. Great forces created her. They shaped her, defined her and, through countless transformations, formed her into a blue jewel. It is her relationship to the sun, the influence of the moon and the protection of the planets surrounding her that have made earth the mother of the solar system. Through her, God's creativity takes form.

And the Lord God formed man from the dust of the ground, and God breathed into him the breath of life and man became a living soul.

All creatures, all the myriad species inhabiting air, land and sea, dwelling in the dark alcoves of caves or watching the world from lofty mountaintops, all are subject to the earth's influence. All feel the ground tremble when the earth adjusts herself. All seek shelter in a storm. All feel the warmth of the sun, the cold of winter, the shifting tides of the seas. In the same moment, she can be extreme and subtle, gentle and violent; nevertheless, the earth supports all who partake of her wisdom.

She neither favors nor discriminates. All creatures that dwell upon her are part of creation. To her, the eagle and housefly are the same. The lion and the lamb have their right to survive.

Roses and poison ivy grow in the same field. Each has adapted to the transformations of the world.

The earth continues to change. She absorbs the wisdom of creation with every shift in the universe. She gathers from space the drifting cosmic particles that hold the memories of falling stars and the histories of ancient planets. She will continue her long journey as an expression of God's creativity until the end when the sun grows cold and fades, when planets and meteors collide and the galaxy once again is transformed into a new manifestation of creation.

Nothing lasts forever. All beginnings have an end. Even so, though your life on earth is temporary, embrace all that she has to offer. She has much to give. The experiences to be had on earth are as innumerable and diverse as the variety of roses throughout the garden. You dwell upon the planet to experience her vast wisdom, to grow and blossom forth in true beauty, expressing the innate possibilities of human potential.

Therefore, be open to experiences that encourage growth and transformation. Like a seed sending roots deep into the soil, seek out that which nourishes not just the body but more importantly, your soul.

Begin by sitting comfortably and quietly without distractions. Play soothing music, if you like. Keep both feet flat on the floor. Barefoot is best, but not necessary. This is an exercise in focusing and expanding your awareness. More than imagination or visualization, this exercise awakens the ability to increase your awareness beyond the margins of familiar physical surroundings.

Breathe deep and relax. Let nothing disturb you. Let nothing be more important than this moment. Direct your attention to the bottom of your feet. In the middle of the soles of your feet are energy fields grounding you to the earth like the roots of a rose. You may feel a tingling sensation in your feet or "see" within your mind an image such as a rose opening its petals.

Like any exercise, it may be uncomfortable in the beginning. Perhaps you'll feel nothing at all. Whatever may be your experience, simply keep your awareness on the soles of your feet. Take time. Focus your attention.

At this point, stop reading. Close your eyes, if you like. Pause for just a few moments and make a concentrated effort to feel the energy where your feet touch the ground. When you feel ready then continue reading.

It takes some effort in the beginning. With practice, like any exercise, it will get easier. While remaining focused on the soles of your feet, begin to expand your awareness into the earth. Go beyond the concrete and asphalt and feel the vibrant energy beneath the surface of the earth, the deep pulsating resonance of nature, the rich minerals of the soil and the vigorous flow of underground rivers. Go deeper into the core of the earth and feel just a fraction of her generative and destructive power.

Draw this energy into you. Like the roots of a rose absorbing nutrients from the earth, allow the energy to disperse throughout your entire being. Let it flow into bones and blood, muscles and organs, into every cell of your body.

Do not fear the earth because she is uncontrollable. Fear causes separation. Instead, feel yourself a part of her, a companion in the intricate grandeur of God's creation. Yes, she can be harsh at times, but the earth also nurtures. She often seems wild and destructive, but such is the force of creation. Better to understand the earth than to fear her. She is neither a paradise nor a hell, but a small expression of God's infinite creativity. Appreciate the earth as a part of creation and realize her form is always evolving. Through natural and human-imposed influences, she transforms accordingly. Better to adapt to her changing nature than resist her wisdom.

Your experiences on earth have much to teach you. Become aware of the cycles of the earth and see within yourself the cyclical seasons of life, the periods of winter's rest, the spring when effort is needed to grow, the gathering time of summer, the sacrifices of autumn. Know that in your life there is day and night, dawn and dusk. Life on earth is cyclical. The planet rotates around the sun, which revolves within the galaxy, but within the natural cycles of life, transformation is constant even when you feel it the least. The challenges and rewards of daily life on earth will strengthen you and help you grow if you remain grounded in wisdom.

Like the roots of a rose clinging to the soil, anchored in the wisdom of the earth so neither wind nor flood can dislodge it, stay firm, determined and strong so neither scorn nor praise can dissuade you from your path. Remember, it is not the words of others that guides you, but the desire to blossom and express your full potential.

Once grounded and firmly rooted in earth's ancient wisdom, other roots spread forth to gather moisture and nutrients. The roots of the rose will reach in any direction to find the minerals and water it needs. Without nourishment, either it will be a sickly stunted plant or it will not grow at all, remaining a dried hollow seed. In order to express its full potential and blossom in beauty, it will overcome any obstacle.

You must also seek out food for your soul. Nourish yourself with daily prayer and meditation, contemplate images that remind you of a greater reality, seek out the writings of those who've discovered and walked the different paths throughout the garden. As you do so, remember such acts alone can do nothing. They must be absorbed, utilized and become an influence in your growth. They must be internalized.

Do not just look upon the earth. Walk. Feel. Experience. Take within yourself her energy. Let her enrich you. Let the earth reveal her history and teach you. Then you will find you can adapt to changing circumstances like the elephants that roam the sand dunes. You will discover you have the persistence and patience needed to blossom even if it takes a hundred years.

You will find on the earth relationships of mutual benefit even from the most unlikely sources like the fungus that aids the rose. And, like the creatures of the sunless ocean depths, you will bring light where once there was only darkness.

Chapter 10 - Water

A rose cannot grow in dry soil. Even though the land is rich in minerals and the climate is temperate, without water the rose will die.

The rose depends on water to dissolve minerals and transmit nutrients into the roots. It is by the blessing of water that the rose can internalize nourishment, convert it into energy and fulfill its life as a rose.

Nearly three quarters of the earth's surface is water. Most of the human body is water. When scientists look for evidence of similar life on distant planets they search for signs of water.

It is the most flexible, formidable and transformative element on earth. During its cyclical journey on the planet, it will take many forms, predominately the salty liquid of the oceans but also the fresh water of lakes and rivers. Lower the temperature, however, and it crystallizes into snow and ice. Raise the temperature and water becomes a vapor sometimes seen as steam, mist and fog but ordinarily indiscernible as it evaporates into the atmosphere.

Water in all its forms exists throughout the universe. It is found in comets and interstellar star-forming clouds. It is the dewdrop on a rose petal and the canyon-carving river, the rain that comes with thunder and lightning, the glaciers hollowing out valleys and carving mountains.

The same water that nourishes the rose is also the scalding steam, pounding hail and the gentle snow that gilds the landscape white.

Within all its forms, water has many attributes. Water is patient as it continually chisels the shoreline in ceaseless waves turning boulders into pebbles. It can be forceful and sudden as a flood breaking levees, overflowing dams, demolishing bridges and sweeping away buildings. It can also be as still and silent as a mountain lake reflecting the world around it like a mirror.

And yet, in all its forms, whether liquid, solid or vapor, no matter how it expresses itself whether raging or gentle, water never loses its essence. It can flow down mountainsides, fall like rain, stand rock solid or become lighter than air; always it is water, always just two atoms of hydrogen and one atom of oxygen.

Add sodium and it becomes salty. Add sugar and water becomes sweet. Pour in toxic chemicals and it becomes poison. Nevertheless, water remains unchanged. It will purify itself. With the aid of sun and wind, water molecules will vibrate at a faster rate. Liquid then becomes ethereal vapor rising above the earth and leaving behind anything not of its own true nature.

The fundamental quality of water is transformation. It can cause great changes with its twofold power of giving and taking away, of nourishing and purifying. Like a rose growing in the desert, you must also seek out the transformational blessing of water. Its power will help you internalize what is needed to grow. Drink the water of transformation. Let it flow into your soul.

Reading and memorizing scriptures, sutras and even this book does little. They are only words.

Robes and medallions do not make you holy, but a sincere person, though dressed in rags, is more radiant than a white rose in sunlight.

Prayers, mantras and chants said out of obligation are nothing more than empty phrases, but one word expressed with the full power and faith of the heart is worth more than a thousand spoken words.

Lighting a candle on an altar has less meaning than a birthday candle on a cake unless one's entire being is devoted to the act of bringing light into the world.

Therefore, as you walk a new path through the garden, it is not enough to marvel at your new surroundings. The new colors, sounds and fragrance must be drawn into your entire being and nourish mind, body and soul.

Many people, either by choice or circumstance, become uprooted and transplanted into a different environment. While everything around them has changed, they have not. Instead, they cling to old beliefs, old feelings and the old ways of walking in the world. For them, change is only an illusion. There is little, if any, growth.

True transformation from seed to flower begins only when your experiences on the new path are internalized and allowed to shape you. As the roots of the rose draws in nutrient-rich water, you also must take in the truth of a greater reality than the road you left behind. Even if the truth is buried deep beneath the surface or hidden like a pearl within the hard shell of an oyster, it can still be found. Though expressed in a language and culture of long ago, it can still be understood. Seek the truth and wherever you find it, drink from it.

Be aware, however, that the truth of divine creation is not always what you are prepared to accept. Most often, truth is what you fear the most.

Have courage. Keep strength and sincerity within your mind, body and soul as you begin this next meditation.

Again, just sit and relax. Ignore any distractions. Leave behind the demands of the world. Take this time for yourself. Remember, taking time for your soul is an act of wisdom.

Start by grounding yourself to the earth. Feel its energy beneath your feet. Pull it upwards into your body. As you do so, let these written words become images flowing into your mind's eyes and "see" yourself in the rose garden. See the many roses surrounding you. Their fragrance is soothing so breathe deep and relax.

Sunlight on the roses brightens their color. Pink petals look soft as silk. The red roses burn vivid like rubies. White roses seem to float in the air. Pale lavender blossoms invite you to go deeper within, relaxing every muscle, calming your mind, letting the complexities of the world evaporate.

Explore this part of the garden. Notice details: the green leaves, the blue sky above, the music of songbirds in the distance. Feel at peace as you walk further along your new path.

Seek and you will soon find a lake; its calm, sun-dappled water shimmering like sliver. Stand upon its shore. Stand besides its still waters. Stand naked without judgment, without either shame or pride. Stand and gaze upon the lake. It isn't big. You can easily see to the other side. But it is deep. Though the water is pure and crystalline clear, though you can peer into its depths, the lakebed cannot be seen. There is no bottom. It is living water without beginning or end.

When you are ready, step forward. Have no fear. The lake is for you alone. Neither fish nor turtle dwells within. There are no rocks to cause you to stumble, no weeds to entangle you. There is only water.

Surrender to it. Sink beneath the surface. You will not drown. Let go of doubt and hesitation. Plunge into the depths and be surrounded by dazzling brightness. Float within the liquid light. Give in to the water of life and let it purify you. Let it encompass you, softly soaking into the pores of your skin.

Let the water flow in your veins and in the marrow of your bones. Let it pour into your spine like a gentle stream. Absorb the water into every organ, into every cell, every molecule and atom. Feel it wash away the soot and dust of daily survival. Feel it heal any wounds of the flesh and all scars on the heart. Anything toxic is washed away——a black ink dissipating into nothing. Any blocks in energy, anything rigid and stifling is tenderly removed, like brown hard clumps of salt dissolving and disappearing.

The sensation may be as calm as a single drop of rain trickling down a window pane, or it may be as intense as a river uprooting a tree.

Whatever you feel, whatever you "see," no matter what you experience, accept and make no effort, make no judgment. Just internalize the experience. Focus your attention on new energies, new possibilities. If you can do nothing more at this time then imagine yourself relaxing in the clear water; that will be enough.

Come to the lake as often as you wish, even if only to wash away the dust of the day from your hands and feet or drink its pure life-nourishing water. The more often you give yourself up to this experience, the deeper the purification and healing. For now, relax and accept whatever may come and let your entire being be bathed and born anew.

"The water I give shall be a perpetual spring within them, watering them forever with eternal life."

When you are ready, slowly drift back to the surface. The sun may seem brighter, the air fresher, even the garden seems different in a way; the roses more vivid, taller, their fragrance stronger. Don't be surprised. You will see the world with new eyes and see yourself in a new light. The transformation is beginning, but there is more, so much more. But now turn your attention back to the ground beneath your feet. Feel the earth's energy still flowing into your physical body. Be aware that you are holding a book. You are back where you started, however, try to allow fresh sensations to remain a part of you.

Sit and relax. Give yourself time before turning the page to the next chapter. Allow yourself time to feel the new growth within you. Be as calm as a lake on a summer's day. Be at peace.

Chapter 11 - Fire

The flickering glow of a candle, the fury of a burning forest, the flare of bursting fireworks; all are visible signs that something is changing.

Fire is the sign of transformation.

It is both the result of change and a catalyst for change.

The strike of a match, the shock of a lightning bolt or the relentless heat of the sun will ignite the spark of transformation. In an split second, molecules are pulled apart, atoms break free of their bonds to realign with other atoms and heat intensives.

The fire begins.

Once started, its energy expands. Change begets change. As long as fire has oxygen, heat and materials to burn, it will spread and its energy will increase.

It generates its own crucial heat, which then begins to alter its surroundings. Large fires can change the weather creating windstorms to draw unto itself an increased airflow to feed and help it grow. Seeking more fuel to burn, it reaches out with floating sparks and explosive fireballs. It can smolder, perhaps for days, perhaps just for a moment, then it flares, burning and transforming all that is dead and dry, anything stagnant and useless.

People see only the devastation, years of barren wasteland of char and ash, stark and still as winter. But with every death there is a resurrection. After winter comes spring.

An old forest may be gone, but sunlight touches the soil where once there were only shadows. New species of plants and animals have the chance to flourish in a new environment. Roses can bloom in places where roses never existed. What was old become new.

Through the transformative energy of fire, sand becomes glass, metal becomes molten in order to be reshaped, and with its heat and light, fire can transform the coldest, darkest night.

Now is the time to face the fire.

Begin as before with your feet firmly on the floor. Ground yourself. Feel the energy of the earth. These meditations are meant to help you in the world, not remove you. Therefore, expand your awareness but stay comfortably in your physical body. Be conscious of the enormous power of the planet under your feet. Let your awareness sink deep as roots tapping into that vibrant energy and drawing it upwards, flowing into your legs and filling your torso. As you feel it rising into your head, concentrate on the middle of your forehead just above the eyes.

Let the energy of the earth stimulate the pineal gland and surrounding area of the brain, that which is called "the third eye." Awaken your innate ability to see beyond the density of physical reality. Should the sensation become uncomfortable, simply focus your attention back on your feet and once again ground yourself. Stay connected to the earth but at the same time allow your vision to expand outward.

Using the mind's "third eye" see yourself surrounded by roses. You are back in the garden. Each time you visit the garden your vision will become sharper. New details will be revealed. New roses will bloom.

Breathe in the fragrance and relax. As you continue to read, let this meditation gently unfold. Be at peace. In this moment, there is no need for any effort at all. Float through the garden. Be carried along by its color and perfume. Let the unseen forces of life within the rose garden carry you to the lake.

Stand beside its still, mirror-like waters. See how it sparkles. Feel its purity. What happens next is up to you.

You may splash the water upon your face and feel its blessings.

Drink from it and be refreshed.

Dive deep into its depths and be cleansed.

Or, all three. The decision is yours. Just take a moment to close your eyes and feel the experience. When you are ready, continue your journey through the garden. Seek and you will find. The fire awaits.

It burns brightly in the distance. Red, orange and yellow flames leap and flare as if in a joyous dance. At its center, however, it burns blue and steady. It is the heart of the fire.

Do not hold back from this divine fire *"cast upon the earth bringing not peace but division."*

This sacred fire illuminates and protects. It also destroys by burning away the darkness, keeping interference at a distance and melting the chains that bind you to the past. Just as fire on earth requires air, heat and fuel, this sacred fire is ignited by the transformational trinity of true desire, devoted determination and a bold willingness to sacrifice.

The stronger those three qualities are within you, the greater the intensity of the fire and its power to transform.

For now, just stand and face the flames. Feel the warmth of the fire. Contemplate the colors of flickering red, the leaping orange, the flaring yellow. Let these words be like fingers of flames burning in front of you, warm, bright and inviting. Do not fear the fire. Yes, it is powerful. It is the fever that scorches infection. It cauterizes open wounds. It turns monumental walls into cinder and dust.

This blaze is also the fire of passion. Smoldering like coals, sparkling like air-borne embers, bursting forth in a devastating conflagration, the fire of passion kindles the heart with love and ignites the soul with one desire——to be united with the beloved. In its brilliant light and intense heat, the fire burns away any obstacles separating you from your creator.

Throw into its flames any attachments that have withered but have not yet died. Give to the fire any images that arise, any memories, any remnants of people past and present imprisoning you within an old way of being. Do not think about what needs to be sacrificed. The heat of the flames will draw the images to the surface of your consciousness.

Do not hesitate to sacrifice even the image of yourself, formed on the old road of illusions, reflected in the mirrored walls of a limited reality. Let layers of your own narrow beliefs about yourself be nothing more than smoke dissipating in the wind.

Be aware, however, that attachments, even the weakest ones, may have tenacious roots. Like weeds, they will cling to the soil and struggle to survive. Each time you stand and face the flames with patience and persistence, the fire will singe another level, eventually burning away even the most deep-rooted weeds.

Yes, the fire burns but do not fear the pain of sacrifice. It burns away just enough at a given time and no more. The fire is only part of a cycle, the transition from old to new. See not an ending, but a new beginning and do not mourn the loss of flowers that never bloom and trees that bear no fruit. Do not fear the flames but stand boldly in their midst.

The sacred fire removes impurities without causing harm. The sacred fire is kindled with wisdom and love.

The task of divine fire is to keep the smoldering cycle of death and rebirth always in balance. Too hot a conflagration causes devastation, burning to a crisp both weeds and roses. Too fast, too sudden a flame is like fireworks beautifully illuminating the night but just for a moment. Then darkness soon returns.

Sacred fire never ends. Its light never fades away. No darkness can overcome it. Its flames burn brighter, higher and hotter than any earthly inferno. It has the power to melt the chains of limitations, destroy walls that imprison the soul and set the heart ablaze with divine desire. This fire of radiant love is eternal, always guiding you deeper into the rose garden and lighting the way along the new path.

Come to the fire as often as needed. Be willing to sacrifice. Find strength within the glowing embers. Keep the fire burning with your devotion.

Then, when you feel ready, step into the flames and be consumed by its love.

Chapter 12 - Air

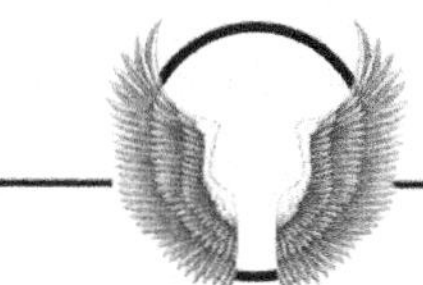

"The wind blows wherever it pleases. You hear its sound, but you don't know where the wind comes from or where it's going. That's the way it is with everyone born of the Spirit."

Unseen, unheard, no scent, no sound; nothing human senses can perceive. Yet, it flows all around you. It exists within you. How much is spirit like the air? Without either, you cease to exist.

The air encompassing the earth is like the Breath of God flowing throughout the universe. Though invisible and silent, it can be known by its cause and effect in the universe. Spirit is revealed just as air is most noticeable by its movement on earth.

It can be seen gently moving as a breeze through the trees, seen in the trembling of their leaves, seen in the rippling waves when the wind sweeps across a lake and in specks of dust floating upon a faint air current through a sunbeam.

It can be heard in the roar of a tornado, the low rumbling of thunder, the creaking groan of tree branches and the rattling of window glass.

It can be felt as a cool breeze when air flows across the surface of the ocean. It can be felt when a strong sudden gust pushes you forward.

Even in stillness, when the air seems heavy, when leaves hang silently limp on the trees, when blades of grass stand rigid, the atmosphere is always moving as it sweeps sand from distant lands, scatters pollen from faraway flowers and gathers ocean mist into clouds.

Though you cannot hear it, the air is always pulsating with sound: billions of voices whispering, shouting, praying and singing; music rippling across the globe. Images surround you, invisibly broadcasted on airwaves. And, with each breath, you draw in drifting particles of ancient stars and planets intermingling with the molecules of air.

Air becomes a visible canvas as light from the sun, the moon, distant fires and streetlamps pervade and tint the atmosphere at sunset in colors as numberless and varied as the grandest rose garden. You may not always feel it, but the air is in constant motion, vibrating with the rapid beating of a hummingbird's wings and the fluttering of newly emerged butterflies migrating across a continent to a place they've never seen.

The movement of air, like the forces of spirit, can be as soft and yielding as a calm breeze then suddenly, unpredictably, the air shifts direction, gathers momentum and hurls a house off its foundations. And yet, for all its power, it is often ignored. Though it constantly surrounds you and flows into you with every unconscious breath taken, it is too often disregarded.

Now take this moment to expand your awareness and, as you read these words, focus on your breathing. Be aware of each breath. Do you take in air through your nose or mouth? Do you feel the rise and fall of your chest? Are your breaths shallow or deep? Did you notice how directing your attention to your breathing caused it to shift?

Conscious awareness initiates change. By simply being attentive to your breathing, you can modify it, vary its patterns and experience different physical reactions. Hyperventilate with short quick breaths and you become lightheaded, perhaps causing an emotional response of anxiety or panic. You can alternate breathing by slowly taking in air through your nose then slowly exhaling through your mouth and induce a feeling of peace, or you can hold your breath until your heart pounds in protest.

For now take slow deep breathes. Focus on inhaling through the nose and exhaling softly through the mouth. Feel your diaphragm rise and your lungs fill with air. Pause for a moment at the end of each inhalation and exhalation. Each breath gives every cell in your body the oxygen it requires for metabolic efficiency. At the same time, with each exhale you expel what is no longer needed in the form of carbon dioxide.

Continue to read as you take in air. Breathe slowly and deeply, expanding your lungs as blood transmits molecules of oxygen throughout your body. Every one of the 50-75 trillion cells of your physical system, through a complex process, uses oxygen to convert nutrients into energy needed to fulfill their purpose. Breathing is a pure and simple action. Though most often an unconscious act, it is an essential part of existence.

So it is with the Breath of God, a constant force always active, always creating and transforming. Though you are unaware of its presence, it surrounds you, is always within you. It is the unseen wind pushing you towards a new path, encouraging you to explore, to experience life in a new way, and giving you the energy to blossom into your full potential.

The new path through the rose garden can be a strenuous journey at times, as difficult as climbing a steep rocky mountain, but the exertion encourages you to breathe deeper, to fill your lungs, to take into your blood and every cell of your being the ever-present Breath of God.

The challenges of walking a new path demands concentration. A new path means a new direction; altering the way you walk, changing the way you think, reaching new understandings, facing new experiences. You have to focus on every step, focus on your surroundings and focus on your feelings. With concentrated focus comes expanded awareness. The spiritual way is nothing more than being aware of what has always been with you. It is becoming aware of the Breath of God that is so crucial to life, yes, even more important than the air in your lungs. The Breath of God gave life to your soul. It made you eternal.

You do not need to earn having the Breath of God in your life, no more than having to make yourself worthy of the air in your lungs. All religions, all scriptures and sutras, every prayer and system of meditation are just tools to facilitate focus. There are other aids to help you feel the Breath of God. Unseen help surrounds you, hovering in the air like water vapor and flower pollen. These angelic forces exist to help you breathe deeper, to energize and transform, to become who you were meant to be and fulfill your destiny on earth.

As you read these words, they draw closer to you. They come bearing roses. Fragrance fills the air. Try to focus. Expand your awareness. Feel them with you. Feel their love.

Relax and breathe deeply. If at this point you are unable to feel the angelic forces enclosing you in scented air created by the beating of their wings, nevertheless, have faith they are with you. They will walk with you along this next step of this journey.

The next step begins as before. Feel the earth beneath you. Remember, a rose pulled from the earth soon shrivels and dies before it can blossom. Therefore, be grounded. Remain rooted in the wisdom and power of creation. Expand your awareness beyond the cold, thick slabs of concrete, the planks of dead wood, the cracked dark asphalt and feel the powerful, vibrant, living earth upon which you walk. As if breathing it in, take the energy into your physical body.

The elements of the earth are also within you. Your body contains approximately the same percentage of water as the earth's surface. The same basic minerals of the earth's crust are also in your body. The same atoms of solid solitary mountains are also within you. At this particular time in space, you share a kinship, a shared existence with the entire planet.

Now, let go of the daily concerns, the routines of survival, the cares and worries of human existence. Step into your rose garden. There is no separation. You and the rose garden are the same. You stand within it, but it is also within you. Among the roses, there is much to be discovered. Within the intricate and mysterious masterpiece of your soul, there is much to be revealed. Focus your attention and, with a new awareness, see a small rosebud, one as small as a grain of rice, a miniature and seemingly insignificant rose, but nonetheless, a valuable element of the garden. With new eyes, you'll see what once was hidden. With new understanding, you'll appreciate the splendor of creation.

Look and see yourself within the rose garden. Notice any new details. Breathe slowly and deeply. Cherish each breath. Feel relaxed and at peace. This is a time to nourish the soul. Just as roses take nourishment from the earth and air and water and the heat of the sun, you must also give to yourself what is needed. Linger for a while in the garden of the soul. Feel its life flowing all around you. Feel the beating of your own heart.

When you feel ready, see yourself walking as if floating on air towards the pure water of the lake. See the clouds reflected in its still waters. Drink from it. Bathe in it. Then wait and feel the water's effect. Again, a deep breath as the water flows through your veins feeding every cell in your body.

After the water comes the fire. Seek the fire of transformation. It burns bright and clean. As you draw closer the flames reach higher, the light brighter, the warmth more inviting. Stand before the flames and contemplate its power. Realize and accept that all things change. Transformation can't be stopped. Yes, you can resist it, but growth and transformation are inevitable. Even the tallest mountain, the hardest rock, the deepest ocean is evolving and transformed by the nature of ever-shifting creation. Only God is constant. Everything else is just a rose petal soaring on the wind.

Now is the time to become that rose petal, to stand in the heat of the flames, to feel the air expand and rise, to feel yourself floating. Your feet lift from the ground. You watch the fire getting smaller. As you rise above the earth, the rose garden becomes a blur of colors. Without any effort at all, you ascend into the clouds. Soft whiteness overcomes you, but just for a moment.

You rise even higher. The clouds drift beneath you. You see the earth get smaller as you soar. There is no boundary to the earth's atmosphere. The air just gets thinner, the blue sky paler as it merges with the infinite universe.

A silent invisible wind whirls around you. The Breath of God lifts you into the night sky. Countless stars burn bright. A small blue planet veiled in wisps of white clouds slowly turns below your feet. Remnants of original planets and primal stars in muted colors of turquoise, ruby and golden amber drift and spiral around you in chaotic beauty, like pollen tossed into the wind. There is no reason for it, no logical sequence of events. Nothing is in a neat orderly formation. How can there be when there are no boundaries, no limitations, where anything is possible? Time and space, explanations and definitions are meaningless where there is no beginning and no end.

The universe just is. God just is. Endless. Limitless. A creator greater than its creation; unbound by words, beyond human logic, defying definition. To try to understand is to struggle. Surrender, however, and you become eternal.

Surrender to the surrounding universe. Be not separate, but feel yourself as a part of it all. Be as a star that transmits light still visible long after the star is gone. Shine that light upon the earth, upon friends and enemies alike, upon all souls known and unknown. It is within you to do so.

Breath deep and feel the Breathe of God. Take it in, feel it flowing throughout your body and soul. Let it be the force powering the light emanating from your heart as you slowly return to earth in your own brilliant luminescence. You continue to descend back into blue skies, into the drifting clouds, slowly stepping back into the rose garden, returning to your life on earth.

Your journey has only begun.

Chapter 13 Deep in the Garden

See the rose garden in all its splendor. See its beauty in bright sunlight and dark storm. See its eternal essence in the blossoms of springtime and the stark bare canes of winter. In every season throughout time, the rose garden endures, always alive, always growing, evolving and expressing itself in multiple forms, surprising colors and fresh fragrances; an intricate filigree of unpredictable possibilities.

Take the narrow path deeper into the garden and discover its mysteries. Walk among the roses and do not fear the thorns. The reward is greater than the danger. The rose garden is vast, boundless, and has much to offer. Sometimes its gifts are simple and easy to obtain. Other gifts are hidden in plain sight, obscured by misconception and false beliefs. Nevertheless, seek and you shall find. Clear away how you think it should be and be willing to discover what the mind cannot conceive.

Though the narrow path seems to meander aimlessly, without logic or purpose, it guides you to these gifts. Follow the path with faith when it brings you to rest upon the soft grassy banks of still waters even when it suddenly curves down into a dark, barren valley or a misty labyrinth to test your skills and determination.

With each step, there is something to be discovered. Every twist and turn in the road reveals a new landscape. Every new rose is a gift. Every challenge strengthens you. Every obstacle is an opportunity.

It won't always be an easy path to walk. There will be the temptation to turn back. You can always return to where you started. The decision is yours. When reaching such a crossroad you have a choice——to return to the road that appears safe, unchallenging and clearly marked on a map drawn by others, or seek new vistas by voyaging beyond the known world to find the rarest rose and breathe in its intoxicating perfume, to feel its soft petals and lose yourself in its dazzling color.

It is a rare rose because it grows upon the summit of a steep mountain where only the courageous venture. The road to the top of the mountain is challenging and there are obstacles. Climbing the mountain will test your desire, shatter false beliefs, rip away illusions, but also set free your innate abilities and awaken your true potential.

The first ordeal begins with you. You must face a towering wall built from stones of fear and doubt. Created by the ego to protect you, it has grown so thick and strong it entraps rather than serves. You must begin to dismantle it, create an opening and boldly step through it.

You will face this wall again with every new challenge and startling experience as the road takes you through unfamiliar territory. As you move forward on your journey, more stones will topple. Eventually the wall diminishes to rubble and, with a single step, you will easily overcome fear and doubt.

The second obstacle is much more difficult. It is complacency. Soft, comfortable, seemingly secure, this wall is a formidable hindrance, more so than fear. Complacency seems harmless, doesn't even appear as a wall, but rather like a welcoming oasis to the weary traveler.

It is only a mirage, a mere illusion generated by the desire for personal safety and physical comfort found in the reassurance of an uninterrupted routine. Complacency is like a potted rose that never grows beyond the confines of its terracotta prison, always hungry, always cut short, never experiencing the depth and expansiveness of the rose garden. Being complacent is accepting a limited reality and grasping for a return to normalcy when unexpected events do arise. Like a mirage beckoning in the distance, the ego's need for security will lead you astray. The more you chase after it, the further away it appears.

True contentment comes from an inner sense of equanimity, an awareness of opposing and complimentary forces and their interaction in an ever-changing universe. There is an inner calmness, an overwhelming feeling of peace, when you accept that the rose must have both sweet-smelling petals and piercing thorns. Fulfillment and purpose comes from accepting the complex forces of God's creativity and simply expressing your own true nature as a component of the Divine Design.

It is by accepting the changes in the seasons you become a part of their natural flow. Adapt to the influence of change and it will awaken the potential within you. Boldly take the narrow path, wherever it may lead, embrace the universal force of creation, and be a part of the wondrous power of God.

Walk with confidence and with faith. The journey will take you along a stony road through a barren wasteland and then lead you through lush meadows of wild roses. There will be mountains to climb and rivers to cross. You will stumble. You will fall. When winter comes and everything is bare and seemingly dead, you will be tempted to give up. With real desire and determination, however, you will rise up and continue your journey. You will overcome any obstacles. You will demolish all walls. Continue to seek and you will obtain the rare rose.

Once you have held the rose and taken its beauty into your heart, it is then you face the greatest challenge of all——believing you have reached your goal, believing your journey has ended because you have reached the pinnacle of achievement. But it is only one rose among many. Another rare rose emerges in the ever-evolving garden. It waits to be discovered. Once found, seek out another and continue gathering roses. Let your arms overflow with all that creation has to offer.

With each new gift another path is revealed, another journey begins. There is more to be discovered, so much more to experience. And, should the narrow path circle back and you return to where you first began, do not be dismayed.

You will see old lands with new eyes and discover mysteries you missed before. You may even meet old friends who want to know where you've been and you will tell them. As proof of your journey, you will offer them the gift of a single rare rose.

Chapter 14 Offering of a Rose

Though it grows in abundance, some people glimpse only a single petal. It blossoms throughout every season, and yet, some people can only perceive a hint of its unique fragrance drifting faint and elusive in the air. It is an eternal rose that never wilts, never dies, but some people can only grasp it for a brief moment before the clamor and cares of the world crush it.

This rose is unlike any other. It has no color because it contains all colors. It is the white rose of purity and innocence, the pink rose of gratitude and appreciation, the yellow rose of joy and friendship, the orange rose of passionate desire, the lavender rose of enchantment and majesty, the deep red rose of self-sacrifice and devoted love.

This absolute, eternal rose is all roses that ever were and ever will be. It is the original rose. Oil from this rose heals all wounds. Its fragrance brings ecstasy. Its wide green leaves embrace and protect. Its sharp thorns can pierce the most hardened heart.

Though everyone seeks this rose, few will admit it. Many, in fact, have ceased to believe it exists. Instead, they gather substitutes of silk and gold, imitations of molded plastic and carved wood. They hold bouquets of weeds and dead wood, or even grasp shards of broken glass just to have something to hold. Not because the true, eternal rose is rare and unobtainable, nor is it hidden. They just don't believe it exists.

Perhaps at one time, they did believe or at least hoped it was true. They were told it promised fulfillment, happiness, security, companionship. Without it, their lives would be empty, so it was implied. For that reason, they waited, but it did not come. They searched, saw it in another's eyes, but it was fleeting. They searched again, but it was nowhere to be found. All the while, the true rose was never far, but blinded by a desire for romance, chasing a cure for loneliness, seeking acceptance, looking for someone to protect and care for them, always searching for someone to give them love, they did not see the rose they sought was within their own hearts.

Planted there a long time ago, hidden among weeds of disappointment and rejection, weakened by parasites of ambition and self-gratification, still the rose grew behind the walls surrounding their hearts.

Many searched throughout the world to find the rose and many sat waiting for it to be delivered, but only the courageous ones were willing to seek the original rose of love offered in the hand of its creator.

The rose of the heart is freely given to all who would accept it. There is no price to pay, no requirements, no obligations. Accepting the offer, however, takes the willingness to demolish all walls, eradicate every weed and let go of anything that may hinder the rose from blossoming in full splendor.

It means relinquishing cherished beliefs that love is a special commodity, a precious and extraordinary bond shared between lovers, a wife and husband, a parent and child. Such expressions of love are only reflections of a greater love, offshoots of the true rose of Sacred Love.

For God's love is an eternal love shinning like the sun upon all roses as it illuminates the entire garden in warmth and radiance. Nothing on earth can lessen its power. Weeds avoid it. Pests flee from it. The four seasons honor it.

Neither storm clouds nor darkest night can cast a shadow and dim the brilliance of the true rose. Neither hurricane winds nor fire's smoke can lessen its fragrance. Neither the judgments of another nor personal condemnation of ancient rules devised by humanity can deny you the offering of this rose. No mistake made in the past can take away the rose of Sacred Love.

Though it is an offering, it is neither a gift nor a reward. You do not need to earn God's love. The eternal true rose has always been yours. All you have to do is feel the love that surrounds you, to accept what has always been with you.

To accept the offering, you must remove all barriers that keep you from accepting what is yours. As walls tumble and weeds are discarded, you clear the way for the rose in your heart to grow beyond the shadows of human constraints, to push through the confusion of a superficial, idealized illusion of love. Without the illusions of what love should be, you can then discover what love can be.

In the light of understanding and compassion, the rose will blossom hundred-fold in luminous color. Roots will extend deep into the very marrow of your bones. Its thorns will pierce through the darkness, shredding illusions and tearing away veils of separation. A sublime perfume will surround you, cleansing the air and soothing the soul. You will walk upon the earth sheltered within its petals and it will remain with you forever. Love is not a gift to be given or taken away. It is not a reward. Love is the motivation for all you do.

Just as it's the nature of the rose to be fragrant, it is the nature of the soul to love. And, as the rose gives freely of its fragrance, regardless of whether or not someone is there to receive and appreciate its perfume, so the soul emanates love, whether or not someone accepts it.

While many seek this love, few reach out and take the offered rose. They fear its thorns. It is the commotion of the human mind, the pain of a broken heart and the protectiveness of the ego that rejects the offering.

Therefore, be forewarned and prepare yourself. The rose of Sacred Love is a formidable power, a threat to the ego, a challenge to selfishness, a destroyer of deception. Of all the forces shaping and transforming the boundless universe and the personal soul, Sacred Love is the most compelling with a power that overwhelms and consumes.

Yes, it can be gentle, nurturing, and healing at times, but it is also a rose that grows beyond the confines of personal desires and expectations. As its petals unfold in your heart, fear may arise as you feel a force you cannot control. You may resist its power as something intrusive, something more powerful than yourself. Understand that, yes, it grows in your heart. Yes, it has always been with you. Nevertheless, you do not own it. You did not create it.

Sacred Love radiates from God through your soul, but it is not yours to command, no more than a rose can direct where the wind carries its fragrance. Spirit is the wind dispersing love into the world. Just as the rose instills the air with its unique perfume, sometimes with a subtle whisper, sometimes with a fragrance so intense that a single blossom can overpower all other flowers, favoring no one, giving to all, so too does the soul infuse the world with love.

Give this love to yourself. Accept the offering. Once the rose of Sacred Love is firmly rooted in your heart, let the wind of your spirit spread its fragrance out into the world. Offer the rose without fear or hesitation.

Chapter 15 What God Said

In the beginning when the earth was young, the rose strived to be a part of creation. Other plants and flowers existed in the past, leaving behind the memory of their life in the deep rich soil. The rose drew upon their history, burst from its seed, took root and sprouted— —small, vulnerable, a new expression of life in a world still shaping and defining itself.

The earth was still adjusting to its new place in the universe, still shifting under the influence of new forces. Seasons were extreme and erratic. Heavy snows crushed down upon the rose. Dry winds pulled at it. The burning sun scorched it. So the rose held tight to the ground, digging deep into the earth, clinging with determination whenever autumn's gale winds threatened to uproot it. In springtime, it grew strong resisting the suffocating weeds and ravenous insects.

Winters were long and harsh but the rose patiently endured. It waited in silence, conserving energy until the sun's fire returned and melted the yoke of snow and ice. Even so, whenever the rose emerged from the darkness and spread its leaves to gather the warmth of springtime, the beasts of the field devoured it. So the rose shed all of its leaves and replaced them with thorns to pierce lips, tongue and throat. Animals quickly learned to avoid it.

Left alone to develop, the rose grew tall and multiplied, spreading its roots from which other roses sprouted. Thickets of roses soon dominated the landscape. Habitable land became scarce. Sunlight became precious as rose competed against rose, each trying to overshadow the other. Thorns became sharper, longer and deadlier. The rose garden became a tangle of jagged spikes—roses slashing roses, each one striving to be the tallest, oldest and most beautiful flower in the garden.

The memory of earlier times, when the rose struggled to survive, was so strong it blotted out all other memories. The rose forgot every rose was an offshoot of the original rose. It forgot how much it depended upon the earth to sustain it. Most of all, the rose no longer remembered how to hear the voice of its Creator.

God whispered in the patter of rain, but the rose was deaf. When the voice spoke in the whirling winds, they clung to the earth and did not listen. In the roar of ocean waves and in the rumble of an earthquake, God called out to roses, but their fearful wailing was louder.

God then sent forth messengers into the garden. Some roses had become such dense hedges of thorns the messengers could not enter. Other roses listened and once again grew leaves to gather in the light, but they also sharpened their thorns, convinced the message they received made them wiser, more beautiful and more loved than any other rose and so needed to protect themselves from jealous adversaries.

God called out again but the rose heard only the clashing of razor-sharp thorns, the cries of the wounded and the low lamentation of the earth as roots carved furrows deep as graves.

So God sent a gardener

to prune away dead branches

but the roses became angry.

to travel throughout the garden,

speaking to every rose no matter how old, how big or how strong,

but the roses became jealous.

to trample the weeds and uproot them,

but the roses became apprehensive, afraid they would be next.

to remind them of the original rose, to awaken their deepest memories,

but the roses were obstinate.

"We have no need for a gardener," they shouted. "Our thorns are our survival."

The roses lashed out in fear and anger. Thorns pierced the gardener's hands, feet and side. His blood fell upon the earth, seeping into the dirt where it remained a perpetual reminder.

Years passed and the roses continued to grow, continued to battle, continued to cling to the single memory of harsh survival when the earth was young. Some roses, however, spread their roots into the blood-soaked soil and drank from it. Older memories were nourished by it. The roses began to remember.

As the ancient memories surfaced, the roses began to hear a voice echoing throughout the universe. Faint at first, but the more they drank the more they heard.

And when they heard what God said, they began to laugh.

The roses laughed so hard their hearts burst open and blossomed into flowers of splendid beauty.

What did God say to the rose?

Now that you must find out for yourself.

ABOUT THE AUTHOR

"It's the message not the messenger that is important," Vincent Cole often says. Nevertheless, to satisfy people's curiosity, he offers this statement.

"When people ask me how I came upon the spiritual path, I reply, 'Screaming and kicking all the way.' Before certain experiences led me down a different road, I was everything society rejected and religion judged as wrong. I have no regrets about my 'previous' life. In fact, I admit it was a lot of fun. Most of all it gave to me a greater understanding of life on this planet and a deeper compassion for the struggles of humanity.

But I discovered something better, more meaningful and worthwhile than what the world had to offer. It hasn't been easy and each day I feel as if I am just beginning.

"What I write is simply sharing things I have experienced and to express the simple message that there is more to life than what we've been led to believe. No matter who you are or what you've done in the past or where you come from, there is a path leading to great exploration and wondrous discovery. You just have to take the next step and enter the garden."

Other Titles by Vincent Cole

The Next Step in Evolution – a personal guide.

The Way of the Monk in Everyday life.

Made in the USA
Coppell, TX
06 October 2020

39147247R00105